COWBOY: THE LEGEND

Gino Valentino

authorHOUSE®

AuthorHouse™
1663 Liberty Drive
Bloomington, IN 47403
www.authorhouse.com
Phone: 1-800-839-8640

© 2011 Gino Valentino. All rights reserved.

No part of this book may be reproduced, stored in a retrieval system, or transmitted by any means without the written permission of the author.

First published by AuthorHouse   4/27/2011

ISBN: 978-1-4567-4884-5 (e)
ISBN: 978-1-4567-4885-2 (dj)
ISBN: 978-1-4567-4886-9 (sc)

Library of Congress Control Number: 2011903230

Printed in the United States of America

Any people depicted in stock imagery provided by Thinkstock are models, and such images are being used for illustrative purposes only.
Certain stock imagery © Thinkstock.

This book is printed on acid-free paper.

Because of the dynamic nature of the Internet, any web addresses or links contained in this book may have changed since publication and may no longer be valid. The views expressed in this work are solely those of the author and do not necessarily reflect the views of the publisher, and the publisher hereby disclaims any responsibility for them.

Acknowledgments

Writing a book is a team effort I would like to thank everyone that helped me in writing this book!

Kim Super and **Scott Napier,** Laurie Shepherd and Dee Napier, Angela Fredrickson and Daniel Fortune, Don, Brian and Tom

In Memory of
Raymond D. Ottoboni
Mae Ottoboni
Jack Lantz
Donna Lass
James Campbell
Katie
Windy
Alice

Dedicated to all of the "Zodiac" victims

Contents

I.	The Early Years	1
II.	Politics	4
III.	Gambler	6
IV.	Based On A True Story	9
V.	Zodiac Years	23
VI.	Chief of Police	38
VII.	The Mob	42
VIII.	Nightmares	45
IX.	Fired	48
X.	Arrested	50
XI.	The Miracle	75
XII.	"Cowboy"	81
XIII.	Gambling Syndicate	99
XIV.	Documentary Movie	104
XV.	Tragedy	107
XVI.	End of a legend	130
XVII.	Zodiac Investigations	134
XVIII.	Published Book	146

Introduction

This story begins in a small town, Colma California. It is South of San Francisco, California. Colma is a Cemetery town not many things happen there! The Ottoboni family was a household name. My father Raymond D.Ottoboni was a powerful Politician and a Real Estate Tycoon!

My name is Raymond J. Ottoboni, I followed in my father's footsteps. I was the **youngest councilman** and then the **youngest mayor** in California. When I was a policeman I was always in the local newspapers. Every mistake I made it was in the newspaper! My life was surrounded with ups and downs, like a merry-go-round!

The most **bewildering true story** took place in the 1970's and the 1980's. In 1970 I was a rookie policeman and I was involved with a serial killer! In 1971, I became Chief of Police. In 1972 I was involved with the **mob**! Four years later I was **arrested** in Colma California!

In 1980 I was **elected Councilmen** of Colma. In 1983 I became **Mayor of Colma!** This is totally incredible!

In 1985 I became a multimillionaire and thirteen years later I was broke. **To the reader**, is it possible all the chain of events happened to one individual?

The word **extremist** is a very interesting word. Do you know what it means? Read this story! **Extremist** is a person that is completely **Fucked up!**

The story tells about a man in Reno, Nevada that became a legend! His money, fame and compassion for helping other people was legendary. He became a legend in his own lifetime. He had it all! Money, women and fancy cars. He had a unique way of getting in and out of trouble. This man was known as the **"Cowboy!"** He was the most **Famous individual** in Northern Nevada!

This story is continuously reminiscing into the past! I tried to stop thinking about what happened back then, but my mind is weak. I started thinking about the "Zodiac" days. I had Flashbacks during the days of the Cowboy's era. It made me feel powerful! I ended up broke in late 1998. Later in the years, the flashbacks became more terrifying and the nightmares became more realistic!

The torment of that day in Lake Tahoe in 1970 is punishment enough. The sin of that night will haunt me continuously. In some twisted way, my mind suggests that somehow I am to blame.

When the mob approached me in 1972, I did what I thought was right! I am not sorry for the decision I made. My family was in danger so I had no other choice.

I wrote a book in 2009 about the "Zodiac" serial killer. The police departments that were involved in the "Zodiac" case believed I was a fraud. The San Francisco police believed there were two "Zodiacs. One Killing and one writing the letters. In my book I stated there are two "Zodiac" killers, how come they did not believe me? Was there a police cover up? But why? The "Zodiac" Killings were never solved. Today most people are thinking what did happen to the "Zodiac" Killer? Who was he?

Terrible memories of the murder of Donna Lass and my involvement with the "Zodiac" killer and the loss of millions of dollars took its toll on me. In 2001 I changed my name to Gino Valentino.

This story is about an individual from a small town becoming famous for his achievements and his failures.

You the reader, after reading this autobiography you will understand how difficult it was to write about someone you never knew. **Two different people!**

The cowboy struggling to protect **Prostitutes, running away from** their **Pimps! What a story! If you like excitement, this is the story for you. I hope you do not get frightened!**

Chapter I

The Early Years

(1941-1962)

My name is Raymond John Ottoboni. On June 25th 1941 I was born in Children's Hospital in San Francisco, California. I was raised in Colma California. Colma is a small town just south of San Francisco, which is comprised mostly of cemeteries. Having grown up an only child of wealthy parents I had a sheltered childhood. I saw pictures of myself when I was a child. My hair looked like a girl. I was wearing a skirt in the 1940's. I believe it was normal for a male child to wear a skirt.

A dynamic event took place when I was five years old. My father took me in his truck to a popular Italian grocery store. He went in the store, leaving me in the truck. In those days there was no baby seat. It was a long time ago I barely remember what happened. I opened the glove compartment and took out a gun. I thought it was a toy gun. I had the gun turned around and I was looking down the barrel of the gun.

I was trying to press the trigger. I didn't have enough strength in my fingers to pull the trigger. My father was coming out of the grocery store, saw me pointing the gun to my head, he dropped the groceries and opened the passenger door and took the gun away from me. I don't remember what my father said to me, but I was crying because I wanted my toy gun. When I got older my father told me what happened. I know it wasn't my father's fault for having the loaded gun in the glove compartment.

I was born with a birth defect. I had a serious stuttering problem. My parents took me out of elementary school because the other children were making fun of me. I could barely talk! It was awful! My parents hired a tutor to help me from stuttering. My mother was told by a doctor, I would never be normal. Thank God I got better, so I went back to school.

Growing up, I was always with my mother. For many years I slept in the same room with her. The room had twin beds. My mother had an ulcerated leg! She couldn't sleep with my father. I was eighteen and I was still sleeping in the same room with my mother.

At night, she was screaming with pain! I had to rub her leg to relieve the pain. I knew this was abnormal, but my mother needed me, I had to help her!

Sex was never spoken of in my family. I was taught sex was a sin against "God" unless you were married. Can you imagine how fucked up I was?

In the early 1950's my father was a wine maker. I remember jumping up and down on the grapes. The grapes were in a large barrel. Those were the good old days!

My father was also a gun collector. He used to create his own ammunition! My father had a machine that would produce bullets (they were called reloads).You would push the handle down, projecting the bullet into the casing. That's how a cartridge is made!

Let's talk about the famous shooting range. It was located on Hillside Blvd. in Colma, California. My father rented the range from Olviet Cemetery.

My father knew all the Sheriffs, Police Chiefs and Mayors in San Mateo County and San Francisco. Many famous people went there to practice with their firearms! They were Willie Mays, Willie McCovey , Football Legend, Bob St.Clair and the famous Mayor of San Francisco Joe Alioto. (there were rumors that Mayor Alito was associated with the mob)

My father had a florist shop and six large greenhouses, which he grew many different flowers.**My father was a great pistol shooter**! In the 1930's and 1940's, Harry Jacobs was the best pistol shooter in California, my father was the second best! **That is unbelievable**. I saw pictures of my father standing on a horse shooting at a target. No one ever beat my father in the tournaments at his shooting range. No matter how good you are there's always someone better!

In 1955 I went to Serra High School in San Mateo California. I skipped two grades in elementary School. I started high school when I was fourteen years old! The Catholic priests started me gambling, that was my demise! In 1958, my senior year I owed two priests one thousand dollars. I was only sixteen years old. They wouldn't graduate me unless my parents paid the two priests the money I owed them! I was at fault not the priests. I love to gamble! That destroyed my life forever, throughout my life I lost millions of dollars.

Later in 1959, I got expelled from City College of San Francisco for gambling with the students. They said I was a bad influence on the students!

In 1959 I got a letter from the Draft Board. I was very religious, and I couldn't kill anyone! My father knew Mr. Chase who was the head of the draft board. I don't know what my father did, but I never got drafted.

Later in 1959 I went in the Seminary to become a Catholic priest but it didn't work out, so I quit. **Does the reader** think I made a mistake? I think I did!

I met Jenny in 1959, after one year of dating we got married. We were both catholic so we were married in Holy Angel's Church in Colma California, on our honeymoon we went to Los Angeles. That night was a nightmare! Jenny was a virgin and so was I. The next day we were still virgins. I was inexperienced and she was scared. I wish I stayed in the seminary.

The only reason I got married was my mother wanted a grandchild! The worst was yet to come. She couldn't have children! Jenny was a good person, but the marriage was doomed. In 1962 we were separated.

In 2010, I met someone I knew back in 1986.

Back then he was the manager of Bally's sport casino. He said I was a lucky man!

I was speechless. When I got myself under control, I said are you talking about?" He also stated the FBI approached him asking questions about me. He said they were going arrest me! I was getting paranoid and didn't want to talk anymore about it. I thanked him for the information he gave me. After that he told me slowly walked away! It didn't take me very long to realize, he was telling the truth.

Chapter II

Politics

(1963-1969)

In,1963, I was mentally exhausted. Jennie was begging me to come back but it was too late! It wasn't because I had another woman! I told her I hated being married! Every time I saw her she was crying. I felt bad and hated myself. I wasn't a womanizer! Jennie was the first woman I dated. I was very shy! I also felt uncomfortable with women!

In the winter of 1963 my father told me he wanted me in politics. My father never asked me to do anything, he ordered me! I told him I hated politics. A father and son on the town council! **That's impossible**! My father never understood the word "NO"! I had no other choice! I knew I was going to lose! I put my nomination papers in as a candidate in the 1964 election. There were seven candidates running for three seats, plus I was running against the Mayor! The Last month before election night I was in a state of confusion. I didn't want to win! But I knew this election would make the family name more powerful, therefore I wanted to win. Boy was I messed up! I came in first place! I was happy for my father. **We were the first father and son councilmen in Northern California**. I became the **youngest councilman** in California! I was 22 years old. Even if Colma is a very small town, that night I made **California History**! Everybody was congratulating me, but I knew they hated me and my father. Most of the people that shook my hand voted against me. The bad news is I have to put up with this bullshit! My father warned me I had to stay out of trouble! Naturally, I never stopped betting with bookies.

From 1964 to 1966 I dated many women, never drank alcohol, or used any drugs! In 1967 I met Linda. We got along okay. She wanted me to stop gambling. I told her I would try. In 1968 we were still dating and I was still gambling with bookies! I couldn't stop! It was in my blood. I was a sick son of a bitch!

Later in 1968 I became mayor of Colma, I was 26 years old. I was the **youngest mayor** in California! Colma was just a small cemetery town but I made **California history** again! My picture was in the newspapers. The Daly City Record was the local newspaper in Colma, which was in San Mateo County. That county was the largest in Northern California.

In 1969 Linda and I were married in Linda's church. I couldn't get married in the Catholic Church because I was a divorced man. The marriage was doomed. I was never married to any of my wives! I was always married to my mother! I was a compulsive gambler. Later I got involved with a Serial Killer, and three years later, I got involved with the Mob! I always felt sorry for Linda!

Later in 1969 my father approached me, telling me the town of Colma was going to hire a policeman to assist the Chief of Police (Dino Lagomarsno) he also told me Colma has never had a Policeman attend a Police Academy I told my dad, I'm very religious and I couldn't kill anyone! In an angry tone of voice my father replied ,"This is an easy job." I couldn't control myself anymore, I was yelling at him. I asked him who is going to train me, Dino doesn't know anything about police work! This is going to be a fucking nightmare! No I don't want to be a cop; you know everybody is going to be watching me! Please Dad! I'm going to be a target for all your enemies. My father didn't understand what I was saying. So I gave in and told him I would take the job.

Chapter III

Gambler

Since I started gambling with the catholic priests in 1957, fifty three years of gambling, it's hard to believe it's been that long. I don't know what made me continue! I have no answer. I remember one night I was going to high school. I climbed out the bedroom window and went in the garage and listen to the baseball game in my father's car. My parents never caught me.

Gambling just took me over! Every minute of the day I thought only of gambling. It affected me in school! It got me kicked out of City College of San Francisco and Healds Business College! Any addiction is terrible, but this was destroying my life. I gambled on everything, even when I played basketball and baseball. Believe it or not, when I gamble on myself I won! When I bet on the ballgame which I have no control of I lost. I thought if I went into the seminary to be a priest, I would stop gambling. I only lasted 3 months in the seminary. I couldn't take all the confinement, and I missed gambling.

I got married which was a mistake. Since I got out of the seminary, I always had a bookie. I was always in debt to my bookie and I had no money. My parents always bailed me out. My first wife couldn't have kids, so we got separated for 3 years, so we got a divorce in 1965! I was a playboy for two years. During the three years I was separated I was a playboy, fucking every woman in sight. But my love was still gambling. I remember having sex with a beautiful woman, and my mind was on the baseball game! She got up and went home! I was mad, but gambling was my girlfriend! If **you the reader** think I was a sick compulsive gambler, just wait I get worse, especially when I move to Reno Nevada. So if you want to read about a **tremendous gambler** that **shocked Reno, Nevada** you have to wait.

I got married the second time, Linda knew I was a compulsive gambler. I felt sorry for Linda, she was a good wife and a good woman. I forgot to mention Linda and I had two children Pam and Ray Jr.

In 1970 I was a Policeman in Colma, still betting with bookmakers! The marriage had no chance from the start. I was always in debt! How can a woman stay with her husband when he has major gambling problems, is involved with a serial killer and in 1972 was involved with the mob!

My gambling escalated so bad that I wasn't even doing my job. The Chief of police didn't care what I did! He told me to just write speeding tickets and be presentable to the public. I was making six hundred a month, and losing twice that much gambling. (betting sports) . My parents were paying my debts! It wasn't out of control yet! Just wait!

When I became chief of police in December of 1971, my gambling got worse. My salary as chief of police was eight hundreds per month.

You the reader must understand that a compulsive gambler has no control of his gambling. By gambling I forgot what I did in Lake Tahoe with the Zodiac Killer. I'm not making any excuses! Gambling doesn't solve my problems it makes the situation worse.

My Parents were giving me ten to twenty thousand dollars a month to pay the bookie. If they didn't pay my debts my wife and daughter would of been hurt! The bookie took my bets because they knew my parents were rich. I felt sorry for putting my parents through this fucking nightmare! The addiction of gambling is worse than being an alcoholic or doing drugs. You don't believe me do ya? Being an alcoholic or a drug addict is a physical problem. Sometimes it becomes mental but gambling is all mental. Wait a minute, I'm not finished! Alcohol and drugs can kill you. Gambling doesn't kill you, the gambler just suffers until he or she dies! Before you make your decision, just think of what I said! I was a sick compulsive gambler and the worst thing of all, I don't know how I got this fucken disease!

Now we come to the event that made me sick to the stomach. On major holidays the town of Colma hires extra reserves to direct traffic next to each cemetery. There was about twenty reserves, they got paid for doing this job. The Chief of police gets the money before hand and paid the reserves before they go home. **You the reader** know what happens next! You are spoiling the ending!

I don't remember what the town of Colma gave the reserves. Anyway I lost all the money at the Bay Meadows racetrack. By the way I went to the race- track in the **police vehicle**! Now how do I get out of this mess? **You sick mother fucker**! Naturally, I went to my mother and told her I lost the money from my coat pocket! I knew she didn't believe me! I couldn't tell her I lost the money at the racetrack. My mother gave me a lots of money, I mean thousands of dollars! Many times my mother and I went to the bank and she gave me twenty thousand dollars to pay book makers. On Sunday I paid the reserves. As chief of police I should of known better, I committed a crime, but it's only a crime if you get caught! I am not a thief! I knew my mother would have bailed me out, so I don't consider that stealing! If it wasn't for my parents giving me money that I owed bookies, I wouldn't be alive today! I put my parents through hell, and I regret what I did. That fucken disease is brutal! I tried to quit many times. But I always came back to gambling! It was always my escape from reality!

When I was on duty watching for speeders on El Camino Real, that was the main street in Colma. I had the radar gun ready for the speeders, but didn't give many tickets. I was too busy listening to the radio! Again my gambling affected my work!

Let me end this chapter by saying "my parents gave me approximately five hundred thousand dollars before they died!" This was all in gambling debts. I am deeply sorry for the pain and suffering I gave my parents. When you come to the three chapters of "Cowboy" you will understand what I mean!

Chapter Iv

Based On A True Story

Policeman (1970)

It was January of 1970, my father insisted that I take the job as a police officer. I didn't want to be a cop. I was a spoiled rich kid, also I was worried that I might get killed, anyway I gave in and took the job. My father left me no choice in the matter. I went to the police academy in San Mateo, California on Monday to Friday and worked as a policeman on the weekends. Each day I was at the police academy it was like a prison sentence. I was the only policeman from Colma that had ever gone to the Academy and it was a living hell. The policeman ridiculed me that Colma had only two policeman and they named me the Cop of the Dead. Later I went to the FBI school in San Bruno, California for training in investigations.

In 1970 there were only two police officers in the small town of Colma, Dino Lagomarsino and myself.

Dino was chief of police, but he had no training in police work. It was an appointed position. He and I worked Monday through Friday on the day shift and Broadmoor Police Department was contracted by Colma to patrol in the evenings and on the weekends. Broadmoor was not city, it was unincorporated Colma. My job as a policeman was a nightmare. Everything I did was under constant scrutiny by my father's enemies of which he had many. My duties as a Colma police officer were escorting funeral processions, writing speeding tickets and attending to the scenes of traffic accidents. At accident scenes I would determine if anyone needed to be cited for causing the accident and if there was a need to call Mercy ambulance to attend injuries.

I didn't want to write about what transpired between me and the chief of police, but I wanted **the reader** to know all the agony I went through! Many times on duty in my police vehicle I took Dino to a house. It was located on Arlington in South San Francisco, California. I knew why I took Dino to the house, and that bothered me, but he is my boss! If anyone found out I was taking Dino to see a woman, especially in the police car both our jobs would be in jeopardy. I felt like a pimp!

The story you are going to read is true but I have no physical evidence. I knew the "Zodiac killer", but I can't prove it! The police don't care, because to many people are saying that they know who the "Zodiac" killer was. So the police do not believe anyone! **You the reader**, make your own decision. Don't be scared!

One day in the spring of 1970 started a chain of events that would change my life forever. I was at the scene of a one car accident on Mission Street. The car had gone off the side of the road and hit a telephone pole, sending the driver to the windshield (hardly anybody wore seatbelts in those days even if their car was equipped with them). So, I got on the radio and called for Mercy ambulance. They had the contract for all the Colma/Daly City area. One paramedic and a driver who had no medical training manned the ambulances. That was the fatal day that I met Wayne Messier, who was the Mercy ambulance driver that responded to the call. Wayne stood about 5'8" or 5'9". He was a husky man with a nondescript face. He walked with a limp as a result of a birth defect. He asked me about my gun, a Colt 357 Magnum with Pearl grips. He was impressed with the fancy grips. He mentioned that he didn't have any place to go shooting ,so I told him about my father's shooting range and invited him to come check it out.

Three days later we went to the range. He followed me there in a white Chevy Impala. When he got out of the car I couldn't believe my eyes. He was dressed in a military uniform head to toe, complete with helmet and shoes (wing walkers). He wore two guns, one on each hip, and a bayonet in a holster behind the right gun. **I can never forget that bayonet**. I could tell that Wayne was very proud of it. It had a wood handle, and as he showed it off to me, he told me that it was handmade! I should have realized then that something was wrong. He handled his guns like a professional. He shot equally well with both hands. He was quite a show off with his talent and he ribbed me about being a better shot than I was.

Two weeks went by and then one day I was working as a police officer at the scene of an automobile accident. I got on the radio and called for an ambulance. That was the second time I met Wayne Messier. Wayne told me that he read about me in the newspaper. I was shocked that he knew a lot about me! He called me "**Junior**", and I told him I hated that name (The newspaper gave me that nick name). I believe it was that day he told me he was an engineer. Naturally, I didn't believe him. That would be almost impossible for anyone to be an engineer and then become an ambulance driver.

During the months we knew each other; somehow he got the idea of setting me up as an accomplice in a murder.

One day when he showed up at the range with a friend that he introduced as Bruce Davis. (Years later during my investigations after Lake Tahoe, I found out that Bruce was a Charles Manson hit man). When I think back on my associations in those days, I can only shake my head with abject wonder at just how naive I really was. I also had a friend there that day that I had known for years before becoming a policeman. I'll call him Joey C. He had a black belt in karate and a very violent temper. He hated almost everybody he met, especially blacks. He always wanted to kick their ass. He had been arrested as a juvenile for killing a black kid. In retrospect the four of us made an astounding group that day. A policeman, a hit man and two psycho killers.

In the summer of 1970, Wayne and his father followed me to my father's shooting range. Both of them wore military outfits. Wayne had a bayonet in a holster, and one pistol on each hip. Wilford was a sergeant in World War II, and he had all his medals on his coat. He had a 45 automatic pistol on his right hip. He looked like General Patton. Wayne also had a 45 automatic pistol and a 9 mm rugger pistol.

Wayne and Wilfred shot like they were in World War II. They had anger and hatred on their faces. I never knew why Wayne wore a bayonet on his hip! Later I found out why!

When we started spending a fair amount of time together and when we were both off-duty we would go out and eat at Lyons restaurant or Joe's of Westlake. He had a very domineering personality and talked to me like I was his slave.

When he demanded my full attention he would stare hard into my eyes and say "I am speaking to you!" This would unnerve me but I was an easy-going person and I would put up with it. Wayne was always saying things trying to shock and impress me. One day he told me that he belonged to the church of Satan. I laughed, "Come on, get serious!" He immediately turned very angry and told me he would prove it. He said he would take me to the church and introduce me to the "Master."

In mid-July, on a Saturday, we were at the shooting range and Wayne suggested that we go to the Church of Satan the next day. I had mixed feelings about going. Being devoutly religious, it gave me the creeps thinking about it, but I was curious. So I said, "okay I'll go with you!"

The next day in my Chevy Malibu, I picked up Wayne at the Broadmoor house and we went to San Francisco to visit the church of Satan. I was scared to go, but I thought I was doing nothing wrong against God. I was only curious what the Satan church was about! I knew Wayne's idea was to convert me to Satanism, but I was a devoted Catholic. I parked the car and we walked to the church. I got an eerie feeling about going in, but I went in anyway.

It was a long time ago, but I haven't forgotten the church of Satan. It was painted black and was located on California Street in San Francisco. I was surprised when I saw the church was packed full of worshipers. After the services, we waited out in front of the church because Wayne wanted to introduce me to Anton LeVay. Mr. LeVay was the founder of the first Church of Satan. He was a powerful man playing the devil in "Rosemary's baby." When he performed in church he wore a black robe and a black mask (devil costume) with goat horns on his head. Around his neck he wore a necklace shaped like a star. The star was upside down. The symbol of Satan is the inverted pentagram with the head of the goat in it.(Two horns pointed defiantly toward heaven and three horns downward representing the Trinity denied). The number (5) is vital in the mark of Satan. In the church the crucifixes hung upside down. The altar is covered in black and the candles are black. The satanic holy water contains a mixture of semen and urine. The Mendes "goat" is a Satanist symbol of the devil. The mass is called the "Black mass." Wayne Messier wore a necklace with a "goat" with horns. Now, let's get back to Anton LeVay. He wore a dark colored robe and he had an air of authority about him. He was tall and lean with a shaved head and a goatee they came to a very sharp point.

When I met Mr. LeVay, Wayne introduced me as a friend of his who was visiting the church for the first time. Wayne told him that I made history by being the youngest mayor ever in California. (Which was true, I was mayor of Colma, in 1968, before I became a policeman.) He was very cordial as he shook my hand and he told me that he had read about me in the papers. I remember that he had a very penetrating gaze, and a shiver went up my spine when he looked at me. As other people started gathering around trying to get his attention he said that he was pleased to meet me and hope that I would come again. I never did. It was a scary experience and having satisfied my curiosity about it, I had no reason or desire to go again. In 1975 the church of Satan suffered a serious loss of members; the headquarters remained in San Francisco. Anton LeVay became inactive and then went into seclusion. LeVay suffered from heart problems for years, he died on October 30, 1997, at the age of 67. He was a legend of his time.

The next day I told my mother that I had gone there. I always told my mother everything. She told my father and he exploded with rage. He said to me, "How stupid can you be? If someone saw you there it would have been in all the papers that you are a Satan worshiper. You would have brought disgrace on our family name you fucking bum." I told him I was sorry and I was never going back again.

When I went back to work, I was so confused about my life! Why am I associating with the Wayne? He worships the devil and that could be dangerous for me. Bad thoughts were going through my mind. Wayne is all messed up, and he is going to make me like him. I am afraid of him, but I have to find out why he knows a lot about me. All that week I was thinking that probably he just needed a friend. Wayne was a loner, like me. Wayne hated everybody, especially cops. But why is he friendly towards me? After that week past I forgot all the bad thoughts, and I felt better about myself.

The next time I saw Wayne was at the donut shop, which was located on El Camino Real in Broadmoor. Wayne and the ambulance driver were taking a break from the job. Every day I stopped at the donut shop during work hours. Wayne approached me and asked if I wanted to go to lunch at Joe's of Westlake tomorrow? (Joe's of Westlake is located in Daly City, California.) Tomorrow, being Saturday (I don't work on weekends and neither did Wayne.) I stated, "Where do I pick you up and what time?" Wayne replied, "11 am at Broadmoor house." I smiled and replied, "I'll be there." I left the donut shop thinking Wayne was just a lonely man. A chill went up my spine when I thought of what my father told me. He warned me over and over, "Be careful of someone trying to get you in trouble!"

All the neighboring police departments wanted me out of the police department. They hated my father, obviously they hated me. So I had to be cautious, my father had many enemies. That is why I didn't want to be a policeman. I was never afraid that Wayne would frame me. There wasn't any reason for him to devise a plot against me. I always thought that Wayne wanted something from me. But what could it be?

The next day we had lunch at Joe's of Westlake, I noticed that Wayne never has an appetite, and he coughs constantly. Wayne was in bad shape, he hardly ever ate, and he had trouble sleeping. Two weeks passed by, and every day I thought of Wayne and how fucked up he was. Wayne never talked about women, including his mother. I've never met a person like Wayne! I was concerned that he read about me in the newspaper. I was scared he was stalking me! What is wrong with me? I'm being paranoid!

In the middle of August we went to the shooting range Wayne wore his combat uniform, two guns and a bayonet. He reminded me of a hunter looking for an animal to kill! I got that feeling I was the animal. I immediately erased that thought from my mind and then we started pistol shooting. Wayne started talking about his father bragging about how many soldiers he killed in World War II. Wayne told me he always wanted to be like his father (later on I found out why!) All of a sudden, he said something that I have never forgotten! "I wanted to be like you. I read about you in the newspaper, you were the youngest mayor in California, and someday you will be Chief of Police." I was shocked that he knew that! In an unhappy tone I replied, "so what! You know I hate being a cop." Wayne smiled and said, "That's why I like you." When we finished at the shooting range we went our separate ways. I know something is wrong with Wayne, but I don't know what it was! Wayne told me he was scared of dying. By God, he is only 28 years old! Why is he thinking about dying(later on I found out Wayne was dying of a fatal disease.) I felt sorry for Wayne.

When I arrived home, I realize my police (pig) wristwatch was missing. (That watch was popular in the early 70s.) I remembered I left it on the bench at the shooting range. I went back to get it, but it was not there! I was very depressed so the next day I got another police (pig) wristwatch. (Later I discovered what happened to my wristwatch!)

During the next two weeks I saw Wayne once, and that was at work. I was dispatched to a traffic accident on El Camino Real and someone was injured. I immediately called Mercy ambulance. When the ambulance arrived Wayne and the paramedic assisted the injured male. After they put that person in the ambulance, Wayne told me he wanted to see me. I could see he was very depressed. I told him I'll pick him up at Broadmoor house (Wayne's second home) at 7 PM.

That night I picked up Wayne and we went to Lyons restaurant on John Daly Boulevard in Daly City, California. He wanted to purchase a pistol from my father. I told him, you don't have to pay for the pistol, what caliber do you want? He replied, "a 45 automatic pistol." I stated, "no problem! My father is a gun collector." (My father owns approximately 150 guns and rifles.) The next day I gave him the 45 automatic pistol. I never asked him what he wanted the pistol for! Wayne was always concerned about his father's health. He told me his father had been going to Letterman Hospital, a military hospital located at the Presidio in San Francisco. I can see why Wayne was depressed. After I took Wayne home, a thought went through my mind. His father lived in Sacramento, what was he doing in San Francisco? I found out later that his father lived in many cities.

Wayne called me on Friday night, September 4, 1970. It was Labor Day weekend. He asked me if I could drive him to Lake Tahoe on Saturday. I told him that I couldn't go because my wife was pregnant and it was a holiday weekend. He said it would be a quick trip and we would come back the same day. I asked him why he needed to go to Tahoe and he told me that he was going to meet a friend there. He said it was very important and that he didn't want to drive because long drive gives him migraine headaches. He was not in good health. He always complained of being nauseous and short of breath. I gave in and said that I would drive him.

I told my wife Linda, that I was going to drive Wayne to Lake Tahoe on Saturday and that I would be back that night. Linda did not like Wayne, she always told me that he would get me in trouble someday. I had a bad feeling about that trip. I went over to my mother's house and told her I was taking the ambulance driver Wayne to Tahoe to visit his friend. My mother was scared. She didn't like Wayne, nobody liked Wayne. She told me not to go. She said that I should be with her on Labor Day weekend. I told her that I was already committed, I had to go. She said that it didn't sound right, but if I was going to go I should be careful and not get in any trouble.

I left Saturday morning knowing that I should not go on this trip. Was God telling me not to go? In retrospect, I really believe that he was. I felt very nervous that morning so I took my valium with me. I picked Wayne up at the house in Broadmoor.(This was his second home, the first one being Mercy ambulance where he slept most of the time) I was in my personal car, a white 1968 Chevy Malibu. Wayne had to tell me how to get to Tahoe because I've never been there before. I had an uneasy feeling that I was doing something wrong, a premonition that something evil was going to happen, but I continued to drive. To make matters worse, Wayne started talking angrily about some woman. He said, "I am going to kill that bitch!" Wayne hated women, so I thought he was just shooting his mouth off and I didn't think much more about it. How was I supposed to know that he was confessing to me? My god! Why didn't I turn around and go back to Colma, but I continued on.

We turned off Highway 50, went a block or two and came to a "T" in the road. I remember seeing a street sign, but I didn't remember the name of the street. Wayne told me to turn right and stop in front of the third house. It was a beige one-story with a one car garage on the left. I started to pull into the driveway and he yelled "No, park out there on the street." At the time I wondered why he didn't want me to park in the driveway later I found out why! We walked up to the door and Wayne knocked. The person who opened the door was Bruce Davis. (I had met him before at the shooting range.) I thought to myself, "What the hell was Bruce doing here?" As we entered the house I saw there was a hippie girl with Bruce. I didn't remember her name. **she** didn't talk much.

There was no wall between the living room and the kitchen. There was a long green sofa facing the front door, which served as a divider for the two rooms. To the right of the sofa was a matching green armchair. On the left wall was the door that led to the garage and beyond, it was the bathroom and a small bedroom. On the right wall by the front door there was a cuckoo clock, in the center was a large picture of Charles Manson.(It was the same picture that I had seen on the living room wall in Wayne's house in Broadmoor.) I felt very uncomfortable and I thought to myself, "What the hell am I doing here!" Everyone in the house was a Manson follower except me. We sat around just bullshitting and watching television.

Later on in the afternoon Bruce and the hippie girl went to the store to get something to eat. After they left the house I asked Wayne "is Bruce the friend that you came up here to meet?" He replied "no, I'm going to meet him later." Whatever his business was up here in Tahoe, he was keeping it close to the chest and given me only minimal information.

After being gone for about two hours, Bruce and the girl finally came back with some food. We were all very hungry and we gobbled it all up pretty quickly. Then it was more television and idle conversation, but Wayne didn't participate much. He had become very quiet and withdrawn.

I remember Wayne changing into his combat uniform and at

approximately 10 o'clock Wayne told me that he was going to meet someone and would be back in about an hour. I said "what are you talking about? It's late I have to go home, my wife is expecting me." He told me just to relax and he would be back soon. Then he, Bruce and the girl left together and I heard a car pull out of the garage.

For some unknown reason I felt very scared and confused. I sat down on the sofa and tried to sort through my feelings of impending doom. I'm through, "I can't even leave. I really have no idea where I am and no idea how to get home. I need Wayne to show me the way." If I had only just went ahead and left anyway, everything would have been different. The terrible nightmare that has been haunting me all my life would never have happened.

I fell asleep on the sofa and woke up about midnight, still feeling that something bad is going to happen. I called my mother and told her where I was. She asked me, "what are you still doing there? Are you in trouble?" I told her that I was calling to let her know that I was okay. I asked her to call my wife and told her that I will be late, and be sure and tell her that I am with Wayne and not with a woman. My wife, Linda was a very jealous woman. After the phone call I turned on the television, but I was too nervous to watch any programs. I paced back and forth in the living room thinking, "what the hell am I doing here!" I was getting scared and I knew something was wrong. Now I realize I never should have taken Wayne to Lake Tahoe. I was getting sick to my stomach, so I went to the kitchen to get a drink of water and then I went back to sleep on the sofa.

I was awakened when Wayne opened the front door and came in alone. I looked at my police watch; it was 4 o'clock in the morning. I was angry and annoyed. I said to him, "where in the hell have you been? It's late! He totally ignored me. Without saying a word, he just walked over to the sofa and sat down. Being very upset now, I was yelling when I asked him, "where is Bruce and the girl?" He looked up at me and he replied, "They went home!" I was flabbergasted. I couldn't believe the way his demeanor was conveying a "tough shit if you are upset" attitude. I said "let's go, I have to get home before I get in more trouble with my wife." He just looked at me with a sardonic grin on his face and sarcastically said "I brought something for you, go outside and open the garage door and look in the trunk of the car." I couldn't imagine what he was referring to. I said "What are you talking about? " He didn't answer me.

He just sat there staring at me with a crazed look in his eyes. I knew something was very wrong and this guy was scaring the hell out of me. I put my coat on over my off-duty pistol, a 38 colt revolver that I wore in a belt holster on my right hip, and went out the front door. When I opened the garage door I saw a small hatchback car. It's been so long now that I don't remember what kind of car it was, but I think it may have been a ford pinto. I opened the back of the car and I saw something fairly large that was wrapped in the dark brown blanket. All of a sudden my entire body broke out in goose bumps and I started trembling. I was scared to death. I already fear that I knew what was wrapped in that blanket. I slowly reached over and gingerly pulled back the blanket and my heart leaped up into my throat. It was the body of woman dressed in white. I started choking and most desperately trying not to throw up. I immediately threw the blanket back over her and slammed the hatch closed. I closed the garage door and had to lean against it, trying to catch my breath. I was hyperventilating. I ran to the front door, hysterical and in shock. I pulled out my off-duty gun and crashed through the door. Wayne was calmly sitting on the sofa, still with that crazy grin on his face. I approached him, holding my gun with both hands in a tripod position. I had it pointed at his head. I was screaming at the top of my lungs, "you crazy son of a bitch! You kill that woman and now I'm going to kill you!" He nonchalantly sat back further in the sofa and said, "go ahead and shoot me if you can. You haven't got the guts, Junior!"

This made me instantly angrier and I lashed out with a backhand slap across his face. "Shut the fuck up, you low –life piece of shit!" I realized he was right. Even though I knew this fucker deserved to die. I couldn't just kill him in cold blood. Re-signing myself to this thought, all the air came out of me as I put my gun away and sat down on the other end of the sofa. I was sick to my stomach. I thought of my father and what he told me. "Stay out of trouble and don't disgrace the family name." I wanted to cry but I was so frightened that I couldn't. I had a million thoughts running through my mind. I knew that I needed to calm down a little, so I pulled out my bottle of tranquilizers and dry swallowed two 5 mg. Valiums.

I had to think quickly. Do I Kill the son of a bitch? No, I couldn't do that. Do I call the police? No, that's no good. I'm a police officer and I brought him here and I would be arrested with him. No one would believe me, and my father's name would be disgraced. Should I leave him here? No, that's no good; I would never know what he did with the body I was seriously starting to consider killing him for putting me in this predicament. Wayne calmly says, "if you don't do what I tell you, I will kill you." I was shocked. I have the gun and he's threatening me! I was so frightened; I didn't know what to do. Wayne knows I don't have the guts to kill him, so Wayne got up from the sofa and he insisted that we bury her. I asked Wayne if he knew where we could bury the body. He replied, "Yes, I do! But what are you so nervous about? You're the cop, act accordingly!" I could see that sick fuck was playing cat and mouse with me. This was a game to him and I again thought that I should just put a bullet in his head right then and there. I told him to stand up so I could search him. I patted him down, checking to see if he had any weapons on him, maybe a knife or gun. I had no intention of becoming the next victim. He had no weapons on him. I was thinking to myself that this nightmare was not my fault, so God would understand if I killed the psycho maniac.

We left the house and he drove the car. He turns right out of the garage. We were driving on a two-lane road. It was very dark and I didn't see any other cars. I was trembling badly and extremely nauseous. Two or three times during the drive I thought I would throw up, but somehow managed to control it.

Wayne drove for about 20 to 30 minutes and then without saying anything he suddenly made a U-turn and pulled over on the shoulder of the road. We got out of the car and Wayne opened the trunk. I was afraid to look at her, but no matter how scared I was, I had to check to see if she was breathing. I felt her pulse, there was no heartbeat. Then I knew she was dead. I started to cry, but all of a sudden I got under control. I tried to show Wayne that I was not scared. Wayne saw what I was doing and looked at me with a disgusted kind of sneer on his face, but he just shook his head and didn't say anything. I told him, "I can't touch her head!" So I got back in through the passenger door and crawled in, so I could grab her feet. I can't describe to you how badly I felt at that moment except to say that I truly wanted to die.

We carried the body approximately 50 feet with some difficulty. We almost dropped her. I could barely talk. I was frightened and I wanted to throw up. I was stuttering. As I continued walking, I remember we made a right turn. I believe there was a large body of water. At the time that didn't concern me, I only thought of one thing! Getting out of this mess. This is against humanity. I thought of bringing the body back to the car, but I kept going until we came to an open grave. It was already dug. There were two shovels stuck into the soft soil piled on the side. I again felt sick to my stomach as I realized that this was all planned.

I was being played for a patsy! **This was a total set-up**. But I have to continue to go along until I could figure a way out of it. We laid the body in the grave, although partially dug, the grave was not deep enough. We then took the body out of the grave and laid it on the ground. We dug until the grave was about 3 feet deep and Wayne decided that was deep enough. Finally, I realized that I couldn't continue to do this. I know this is wrong and against God, and all that I believe in. I started to walk away. Wayne started to walk toward me and stated "you got to help me, or you will be in trouble. Remember Junior, you are a police officer!" I turned around and with my hand on my revolver I replied, "you killed her, you bury her!" I immediately thought of killing him and burying them both.

All of a sudden, I was sweating and a thought went running through my mind, so far I didn't kill anyone. Get the hell out of here, you are not a killer. I said, "Okay Wayne, you win, let's get this over with. Wayne slowly walked back to the grave, and I followed him like a baby following his mother. We proceeded to lay the body back in the grave and started to cover it over with loose dirt. I was openly weeping by this time and praying for the poor girl and for God to please forgive me for what I was doing. When we had pushed all the dirt back in the hole, Wayne grabbed both of the shovels and started to walk back to the car. I was still at the grave on my knees crying and praying for forgiveness. Wayne turned around and impatiently said, "come on, let's go! You can't help her now!" I will never forgive myself for what I did that night.

Wayne drove back to the Lake Tahoe house, while he was driving I was so disgusted with myself, I almost made another critical mistake. I took my revolver and pointed it toward his head and told him to pull over. Wayne pulled to the shoulder of the road and stopped the car.

I was yelling at him saying "why did you involve me in this?" "You know I can't get into any trouble. Tell me why you son of a bitch or I'm going to take your head off!" Wayne, calmly looked at me and replied, "Kill me. I'm going to die anyway." While putting my revolver down, I asked him, "What the fuck are you talking about?" Wayne started the car and drove away saying, "It's none of your business." As I put my revolver back in my holster, horrible thoughts were going through my mind, over and over thinking about what happened to that poor girl! I took a deep breath trying to calm myself. Finally Wayne parked the car in the garage and then we left in my Chevy Malibu heading back to Colma, California.

Wayne obviously thought that I was a stupid cop. I saw the license plate on that car. I had an excellent memory back then, Wayne showed no concern whatsoever that I might check up on it. Did he want to be caught? I think that he probably did. But at this point I couldn't afford for that to happen. I couldn't let that happen. If he got caught, I would also be arrested and my father's name would be dragged through the mud. More important still, was the fact that the emotional trauma it would cause my mother would devastate her. I couldn't let that happen.

During the drive back I had a migraine headache and my driving was awful. I was swerving from lane to lane, like a **madman**. I was constantly yelling at him and telling him I was going to find a way to make him pay for what he had done. He was ignoring me and just kept staring out through the windshield at the road ahead. Finally, when I asked him, **"Who killed the woman?"** He turned to look at me and said," you are the cop, you tell me!" Obviously that was not an answer, so I asked him, "What was her name?" He wouldn't tell me her name. His only reply was, "she deserved to die!"

I kept badgering him with questions until he finally relented and told me part of what had happened. He told me that the hippie girl had lured the woman from her car, over to where he and Bruce were waiting. Then he said that he and Bruce killed the woman by strangulation. At that moment I didn't know what to say! I was so frustrated that I couldn't control what I was saying. Then I replied, **"Was the woman molested?"** Wayne stated, "No, I couldn't do that!" I didn't believe him, but it was too late. The woman was dead and what in the hell do I do now?

I pulled over on the shoulder of the road, stopped the car, and said "why did you involve me, I was good to you. I don't deserve this, you are a dead man! Do you understand me?" Wayne replied, "I'm sorry, but I couldn't stop myself." Then he got that wild crazy grin on his face again and angrily stated, "The next one I'm going to kill is that bastard Paul Avery!" I started panicking again at this statement and thought, "Oh dear God, is he completely insane. I have to stop him. At the Colma dump, it's still dark so no one will see me. I can use the unregistered gun that's in my trunk." This thought was immediately followed by, "Oh dear God, I have to put an end to this nightmare. Satan is telling me to kill. I have got to be strong."

Thoughts were running through my head at a million miles a minute, remembering everything that had happened that night. All of a sudden I realized that Wayne had worn gloves when we went to bury the woman. Oh my God! I hadn't worn any gloves. My fingerprints were everywhere. I felt totally defeated as I realized how deep in trouble I was.

Finally, we arrived at the house in Broadmoor. I was totally depressed and I wanted to get even with him. Wayne started to get out of the car, all

Gino Valentino

of a sudden I grabbed him by the shoulder and when he turned around to look at me, I stared hard into his eyes and pointed my finger at him saying, "I'm speaking to you." He never said a word. He just walked away. After that I was positive that somehow he had to die!

Chapter V

Zodiac Years

(1970 – 1971)

I want **the reader** to know the definition of a serial killer.

Serial killers are different from ordinary killers. In several ways they are not political, not domestic and not for profit. Rather they appear to be motivated by rage against some special element. A serial killer is a person who kills more than three victims, at three or more locations, with a cooling – off period in between. A serial killer isn't a monster; he is a human being with a tortured soul. The motive is and irresistible compulsion, fueled by fantasy which may lead to torture, sexual abuse and mutilation. Serial killers like other forms of homicide, are usually one on one. A serial killer is almost always a male. Some serial killers appeared to be completely okay. Most serial killer is complete outsiders, socially inept and complete loners.

Serial killers tend to go on killing until they are apprehended, dies, or are killed. Serial killers are difficult to catch because there is often no prior relationship between the victim and the killer. The serial killer is the most dangerous. He commits hideous crimes and there is no motive or reason why he kills! Therefore the police departments have a difficult time catching him!

This describes the "Zodiac" killer!

The "**zodiac**" and "**Jack the ripper**" are serial killers that are very similar!

Both killers made their own nickname.
Both killers hated women.
Both killers stated in their letters "Catch me if you can!"
Both killers taunted the police with letters and both of them were writing to the newspaper.
Both serial killers wanted to get caught!
Both cases have never been solved!
That's amazing!

It was a Sunday morning when I got back to the house after dropping Wayne off in Broadmoor at the house that I believe was owned by his father. It was Labor Day, a holiday for most people, but unfortunately I had to work. I sat in my car out in front of my house for about 10 or 15 minutes trying to figure out what I was going to tell my wife about why I am getting back from the trip to Tahoe on Sunday morning, when I had originally told her I would be back Saturday night. She was a typical woman. She was very jealous and suspicious of any time that I spent away from her that wasn't work related. She always thought that I was running around with other women and cheating on her, even though that was never the case. I was always faithful to her. I couldn't tell her what had really happened, so without being specific, I told her that I had run into some problems in Lake Tahoe, I also told her that I had handled them and that everything was okay. Linda didn't believe me .She could tell by the way I was acting that I was lying to her and that it was obvious that something was very wrong. She was right of course but I couldn't admit it. I told her "Linda, please just drop it. Everything is fine!" She still didn't believe me but she could see that I wasn't going to tell her anymore, so she left me alone.

The next day I told my mother what had happened in Lake Tahoe. As I've said before, I was very close to my mother and always told her everything. Yes, I know what you're thinking and it's true, I was a mama's boy. When she had heard what I did she became terrified for me and started crying hysterically. This, of course, made me feel even worse than I already did and I couldn't help but start crying right along with her. Through my tears I was saying, "Please stop crying mama. Please forgive me?"

She was inconsolable, rocking back and forth as she cried and repeating, "Oh my God! Oh my God! " She was a strong woman though, after a while she gained control of herself. She started thinking about what could be done about it. She then asked me, "Have you told your father yet? "I told her that I hadn't, that I was afraid to. My father didn't believe in failure. He saw it as weakness and I was terrified of him.I asked her, "Mom, can you tell him for me?" She understood that I was afraid to tell him, afraid of what he would think of me. She told me to go home and then she would talk to him for me.

On Wednesday my father found me while I was at work in my police car. He was livid; his face was almost purple with rage. He told me he didn't believe what I said had happened to me and, "why the fuck are you scaring your mother with this bull shit?" "Who the fuck is this guy you're talking about?" He asked. I told him Wayne was an ambulance driver for Mercy ambulance and that he had seen him at the shooting range. Then I told him the whole story of what had happened in Tahoe. He could tell then, by looking at me that I was not lying about it. When I finished he looked at me with disgust in his eyes. He said, "Holy shit! What the fuck is wrong with you? You are a trained police officer. You should have known this fucking guy was a killer!" "Dad," I said, "How was I supposed to know that a Mercy Ambulance driver is a killer?" His face started turning purple again and he was screaming, "What the fuck are you talking about? You just told me he's a killer. Is this the same guy you are taking along in your police car?" I told him, "Yes, it is!" "Oh, Jesus!" He said. "How stupid can you be?" I just looked at him kind of sadly and didn't say anything because I knew that I had been very stupid. After he calmed down a little he said, "Okay! I'll handle this."

My father was a very powerful man, who had many different connections, legal and illegal. "Please Dad," I said, If he gets caught, I will be arrested and be charged as an accomplice. Please, let me investigate him and I'll let you know what I find out." He didn't like that idea. He wanted to handle it his way, but after some arguing and pleading on my part he agreed to let me investigate and find out what I could.

The next day I started my investigations. I knew that I had to find out who was the owner of the car that Wayne was driving in Lake Tahoe. I had an excellent memory back then so I knew the California plate number, but I couldn't just call it in over my police radio. I needed to be inconspicuous. I decided to enlist my father's help. I had him give the license numbers to the Chief of Police in Colma, Dino Largomarsino. Dino could find out whom the owner was without anyone getting suspicious. It didn't take long at all.

By the end of the day on Tuesday my father got back to me with the information that Dino had acquired for him. The owner of the car was none other than Wayne's father, Wilfred Messier. That didn't shock me too much because I ready knew that Wayne and his father were very close. I was going to investigate Wilfred and see if he was involved. Unfortunately, I decided not to! Wayne idolized his father. Whenever there was the slightest opportunity in any conversation, Wayne would brag about him, his service record and his proficiency as a tree trimmer. Wayne was never in the service and in the short time I knew him he was never in the company of a woman. Wayne hated women, all women. I never once heard him even mention his mother. Thinking about the relationship between Wayne and his father made me wonder if Wilfred Messier was somehow involved in the murders. But how could I prove that without being arrested as an accomplice! I wanted to go and talk to the Lake Tahoe Police Department, but I was terrified of bringing this shame down on my mother and father. I felt abandoned and very alone.

On Friday morning, I didn't want to go to work, but I had to. I went to the Colma police station and kind of wandered around in circles trying to look busy. I was extremely depressed and avoided talking to anyone more than was absolutely necessary. I remember picking up a stack of wanted posters that were on top of one of the file cabinets and started leafing through them. Again just trying to look busy. I came across a San Francisco wanted poster of the "Zodiac." I had read in the newspaper about the "Zodiac" killer but I didn't know anything about him personally. I started reading; the one' description of the "Zodiac" said that he was ambidextrous, walked with a limp, and drove a white Chevy Impala. Oh, my God! This description fits Wayne to a tee! That's impossible, I couldn't believe it. A Mercy ambulance driver could be the "Zodiac" killer? Am I going crazy?

I had to find out more, so I went to Mercy ambulance to see what other information to see what other information I could find on Wayne. I got his application for employment from the woman working in the office. I was in uniform, so she never even questioned me about why I wanted to see it. When I read through the application I didn't see anything that looks questionable or suspicious to me, except that there was no work history listed for him.

He was from Sacramento, California, and is currently living in the Mercy Ambulance building. His father and I were the only people that knew he also had a bed at the Broadmoor house. I found out from Mercy Ambulance Wayne was off on weekends. Later I found out that all of the "Zodiac" killings that took place in Vallejo and Lake Berryessa were on weekends. Also, I found out that the San Francisco cab driver was killed on a holiday and Wayne was off on holidays. After all the information I received from Mercy Ambulance, I still didn't believe that Wayne could be a serial killer, and I never thought a Mercy Ambulance driver was the "Zodiac" serial killer.

I couldn't go to the Broadmoor Police Department to see what they might know about him because they hated me. They wanted my job so they could take over the Colma Police Department. I am still a rookie police officer trying to learn how to survive in a heated small town political situation, and now I am involved in a murder. I was in a highly vulnerable position.

On Saturday, the next weekend I went to San Francisco Police Department. I drove there in my Chevy Malibu and arrived at the Bryant Street police station in the early afternoon. I was so scared walking into the station, I felt like I was about to piss in my pants. If I haven't taken a Valium before leaving Colma, I think I might have. I flashed my off-duty badge to the desk sergeant and told him I was looking for information about Paul Stine, the cab driver that was killed in 1969. I knew from the newspapers that this was the latest "Zodiac" killing. He, of course, was curious why I wanted the information. He was rude and intimidated and obviously felt that I was wasting his time.

I was too scared to tell him anything more. I was trying to say something and then I started to stutter. All my life I always stuttered when I was nervous. I was hoping the Valium would stop this from happening to me, but it wasn't helping. The desk sergeant started to smile a little and I could tell he was about to start laughing at me. This made me mad, so I just said, "Never mind!" I turned around and walked out. I could hear him quietly laughing at my back as I left.

I realized that I wasn't going to get the help and information that I wanted from anyone involved. I decided that I had to investigate this as best as I could on my own. I made up my mind that going back to Lake Tahoe was the best place to start and after week debating this with myself, I built up the nerve that I needed to go there. I would have gone to the FBI, but I was so terrified of what could happen.

I got in touch with a policeman friend, that I had a good working relationship with Charles Feischer(I called him Chuck). Chuck was with the Broadmoor Police Department, but he had always been friendly and helpful to me. We had talked many times about the different aspects of police work. I vaguely told him that I needed to go to the South Lake Tahoe Police Department to check on some things and ask if he could give me directions on how to get there. He said it would be no problem and even wrote the directions down for me to follow.

I took the day off work on a Tuesday and drove up there in my Chevy Malibu. The country that I pass through on the drive up looked familiar to me, as it should have since this turned out to be the same route that Wayne had directed me to take only a week earlier. My nerves was starting to slip and my hands were starting to shake so bad I could hardly hold onto the steering wheel so I pulled over at a wide spot in the road and dry-swallowed two Valiums. By the time I arrived at South Lake Tahoe I was feeling a bit more in control.

I parked and went into the police station. I showed my badge and introduced myself to the officer at the desk and then asked him if they had a missing person. He reached over to the side of his desk, and handed me a missing person poster of Donna Lass. The second I looked at it I recognize the photograph. I had just found out the name of the woman that Wayne and I had buried.

My nerves started jumping around like they were a large string of fireworks going off all through my body. I tried my best to hide this from the officer, but he could see that I was shaken up. He asked me if I knew her. I said, "I don't, but someone I know could have some information about what happened to her. I will get back to you." I asked him if I could keep the poster. When he said that I could, I thanked him and I left the Police Station. I had to restrain myself to keep from running out of the building. By the time I got out to my car I was shaking like a leaf in a high wind and crying like a newborn baby. Luckily, there were very few people around to see me that way. The few people who did see me just looked at me compassionately and kept on walking.

When I got myself under some semblance of control I drove around South Lake Tahoe for a while trying to find the house that Wayne had taken me to. I couldn't find it. I drove around aimlessly, hoping to spot some kind of landmark that I would recognize. I had no luck at all. As I drove back to Colma, I was thinking to myself, "What the hell do I do next?"

I knew what I did in Lake Tahoe was wrong! It was against God. But I can't change what happened! I was scared and wasn't fully aware of what I was doing! I grew up helping my father putting flowers on people's graves. In those days that was sacred for people to put flowers on their beloved one's graves. By depriving the parents of Donna Lass from putting flowers on their daughter's grave will haunt me forever! I am trying to make amends for what I did. Where do I go for help? I can't trust anyone! My father warned me over and over, "Stay out of trouble." Now I'm in deep trouble and there is no way out. If Wayne kills again he's going to get caught. I think I am going to see a priest, I know him and maybe he could help me.

The next two days I went to work but I perform my job listlessly, like I was on autopilot. I avoided contact with anybody else. I didn't even write any speeding tickets although I observed quite a few people driving over the speed limit. When I went home that night, Linda could tell something was wrong and kept asking me what the matter was. She asked me "Was I sick?" I couldn't say this to her but I was all fucked-up. I was sick with regret and desperation over what to do.

I started thinking back to 1970, when I saw the body of a woman dressed in white. My God! That was horrible! Just thinking about that dreadful day, I want to die! If the police don't stop Wayne, I have to! Even if it means killing him. I owe it to Donna Lass.

I decided that I had to confess to my priest what I had done. So I went to Holy Angels Church, which is located on San Pedro Road in Broadmoor. Holy Angels in the church where my parents and I attended Sunday services. I was even baptized there and received my first Holy Communion. Later I served as an altar boy. I was married to my first wife Jenny, in Holy Angels Church, but for the life of me, I can't seem to remember the priest's name. Memory is a strange thing when you get old. There are things like what happened in South Lake Tahoe that I'm sure will never be forgotten. I thought that I was going to be very upset and crying when I was in the confessional booth, but talking about it with a neutral party seemed to calm me.

I confessed everything that had happened up at Tahoe, just as I have related it to you. How I felt the whole thing had been planned to involve me, that Wayne had set me up. The priest never interrupted me, only murmuring an occasional, "Go on my son!" At points where I seem to get stuck. When I was done telling everything, I told the priest how frustrated and angry I felt and that I wanted to kill this man that got me involved in a murder. That was when I realized that the priest knew who I was, despite the confessional screen. He had known my parents and me for many years and I'm guessing that he recognized my voice and the way that I occasionally stuttered while telling him my confession. He said, "No, Raymond you mustn't kill him. Killing is against God's law." I told him, "Father I can't let the police catch him or I will be in trouble.

My mother and father would never forgive me for bringing that kind of disgrace to the family name." I was just starting to think that Wayne might possibly be the "Zodiac" killer, and the police weren't catching him. I told the priest, "I think this man could be the "Zodiac." I heard a little hitch is his breathing through the screen and then he told me to go to the police." That's when I started crying. I said," I can't! I have been set up to look like his accomplice." The priest said in that case I should stay away from him." He didn't reply so I said, "Father you can't tell anyone what I've told you." He assured me that he would not.

He gave me penance and told me to come back and talk to him again before I do anything. I went up to the altar and said my penance. Before leaving the church I went to the memorial candles. I said another prayer and lit a candle for Donna Lass.

For the next few days, I read up on everything I could find about the "Zodiac" killer. The next time I saw Wayne he was at the Broadmoor house. I tracked him down there because I wanted to confront him with what I have found out. We were standing in the living room with that eerie picture of Charles Manson looking down at us. I showed him the missing person poster of Donna Lass. When he saw the poster his face broke into a wide, delighted smile and with an insane look in his eyes he said, "She deserved it. Just like the cab driver." I realized that he was referring to Paul Stine, the cab driver that was murdered in 1969 in San Francisco. I said to him, "what do you mean?" Wayne replied "That bastard insulted me the first time I was in his cab. "You know what happened the second time!" He was smiling and bragging and loving every minute of it, and I was getting very angry. "I do not believe you," I said, "prove to me that you are the Zodiac!"

He walked into another room and when he came back to the living room he was wearing the most evil grin I have ever seen on a human face. He looked even more like Satan then Charles Manson himself. He was pointing with his left hand, crossed his chest and his right hand, which was covered by a black cloth hood that he was spinning around so I could see all sides of it. I had read about the hood and I could feel all the blood draining out of my face as I stood there looking at it. I was scared to touch the hood, but I had to ! I took the hood from his hand and put it over my head. At that moment I felt powerful. A chill went up my spine. Quickly, I had to take the hood off and give it back to him . He was quietly laughing at me. He knew that I didn't dare arrest him because of the way he set me up in Tahoe. He then confessed to me the killings in Vallejo and Lake

Berryessa. Also, he told me he killed 5 more women earlier that year. (He hated women, particularly nurses.) He stated, "You don't believe me, do you?" I replied "No, I don't." I thought he was bragging. (I found out in 2007 Wayne wasn't lying.)

He had complete confidence in himself. I asked him, "Why are you telling me this?" His smile got even bigger when he said to me, "I am going to make you famous someday." He told me the first time he had a urge to kill was in Sherwood Forest. I had never heard of Sherwood Forest, so I asked him where it was? First he told me it was a park in Vallejo that his father had shown him. He told me it was not actually a park, but just an undeveloped area with a lot of eucalyptus trees and that Sherwood Forest was not an official name for the area. He said that the locals who used it as a recreational area dubbed the area Sherwood Forest. Then he said something to me that I will never forget. "I love reading about my accomplishments," he said, Finally, I'm getting the attention I deserve. I can't wait to be alone to relive the sensation of pleasure and power. I am in control and the way that I kill makes me more powerful. All of a sudden Wayne slowly walked toward me and said, "did you ever find you wristwatch?" I replied, "No, how did you know I lost my wristwatch?" He just stared at me, looking like he was angry. Then in a soft tone of voice he replied, "I put your wristwatch in the woman's grave." I was stunned. I didn't know what to say ! I sat down on the chair. There was a cold chill through my body. Finally, I got myself under control and I said, "I don't believe you, I should have killed you at the gravesite!" I got up from the chair and started walking toward the front door. He started laughing and cackling like a lunatic. Which, I decided then he was, not just a killer but also a raving, insane lunatic. I couldn't take anymore. I had to leave. When I walked out the front door I was shaking so badly I nearly fell over as I was walking back to the car.(I never found out if he actually put my wristwatch in Donna Lass's grave!)

Toward the end of that week I was driving southbound on El Camino Real in my police car when I noticed a Broadmoor Police car behind me, and the driver was waving his arm out the window, signaling me to pull over. I made a right turn into the Cypress Lawn Cemetery and stopped at the side of the entrance. I got out of my vehicle and saw that it was Officer Charles Feischer. As I mentioned earlier, Officer Feischer was the only one on the Broadmoor Police Department that was friendly to me. He told me that LT. Baxley, who was with the Broadmoor Police Department, was investigating a Mercy Ambulance driver that has been shooting his mouth off about killing people. Instantly my whole body broke out in goose bumps. I asked, "What is his name, Chuck?" He said, "I don't know! Baxley doesn't tell me anything. We don't get along very well." We talked a little while longer and then said our goodbyes. As he was driving away I started to get scared thinking, "Oh God, I hope Baxley didn't see me with Messier, especially in Lake Tahoe."

I went to see my father that evening to tell him that we had a problem. I told him that Lt. Baxley was investigating Messier and that he had to be stopped. My father, in his violent tone of voice, said "Does he know what you did in Lake Tahoe?" I told him that I did not think so because if Baxley knew that, I would have already been arrested. I knew that Baxley was a good detective, but so far I had luck on my side. He hadn't yet found out that I had been hanging around with Wayne. My father was furious with me, but I knew that he could and would take care of the problem. I stay completely away from Wayne for about a week until my father came to me and told me that Lt. Baxley had been pulled off the case. My father told me that he had gone to the Broadmoor Chief of Police Ray Savage and convinced him to pull Baxley off the case. He wouldn't tell me how he did the convincing and frankly, I didn't care. I could breath easy again.

I went back to keep a watch on Messier because I knew that he was planning to kill again and I couldn't let that happen. Another killing would compound my complexity in his crimes. He had told me, on the Sunday morning drive back from Lake Tahoe that he intended to kill Paul Avery. I didn't know what the connection between him and Avery was, so I did some checking and found out that Paul Avery was a newspaper reporter who worked at the San Francisco Chronicle. Avery was obsessed with finding out whom the "Zodiac" was. He personally believed that he would be the one to reveal the killer's true identity This made me think that Wayne felt that Avery was getting too close and that was reason he wanted to kill him. As far as I was concerned, the reason Wayne wanted to kill him was of no importance. I couldn't let him kill anyone else, under any circumstances.

Later that year, I came home from work and found Linda sitting on the living room sofa crying hysterically. When I asked her what the matter was she told me that she had received phone call that had scared her terribly. She said that a man claimed to be Wayne's father had called and said, "My son is in your husband's police car. Tell him to leave my son alone or I will go to the Chief of Police and tell him that your husband is trying to get Wayne into trouble." Linda was visibly shaken and I could tell that I probably wasn't getting an accurate accounting of the conversation that went on between them, but it makes me very angry that Wilfred would call my wife instead of confronting me with his concerns. I told my wife I would talk to Wayne. This will never happen again! Wayne's father never called my wife again. I believe Wilfred was scared because he was involved!

One day in October of 1970 I went back to Lake Tahoe to see if I could locate the house. I took Highway 50 and I was trying to remember what turn off to take, but I was totally lost. I turned off on a road that looked similar to the one I took in September. I remember seeing water before I parked my car next to the house. I drove around for an hour getting nowhere. "I'm never going to find that house!" I couldn't drive anymore and I was getting depressed, so I gave up and decided to go home. While driving back, I was thinking about Donna Lass. **"Will she ever be found?"**

I drove Wayne to San Francisco in my police vehicle. He wanted to see where the San Francisco Chronicle building was located. While I was driving through San Francisco, I was thinking San Francisco police are after the "Zodiac" killer. So what the hell am I doing with him in my police vehicle? Looking in my rear view mirror, I saw a San Francisco police vehicle flashing its red lights, so I pulled over to the shoulder of the road. I felt ridiculous. I'm driving a police vehicle, why is he pulling me over?

The officer came to my driver's side and asked me, "you were weaving, are you okay?" I started to stutter and very slowly I replied, "Everything is okay, and I apologize for my driving." The officer looked at Wayne and then said to me "Have a good day." I finally realized that I made a big mistake and I couldn't take any more chances. After that scary moment, I went back to Colma and dropped Wayne at the Broadmoor house. Now I know for sure that Wayne had to die. I always dropped Wayne at the house in Broadmoor. I never picked- up or dropped-off Wayne at Mercy Ambulance. I was scared that someone would see me.

When I got back to the police station, Dino, the Chief of Police asked me, " Why did you take someone to San Francisco in the police vehicle, and who was he?" I replied, "he is a friend. I went to San Francisco to get information on a case!" Dino was mad and told me, "Don't go to San Francisco again without my permission." I know I was wrong, but what the hell is Dino going to do to me. My father was a powerful man, and he knew that!

There was one time I thought I was going to die. This happened at the shooting range. When Wayne wore glasses, he looked fearful. They were thick-rimmed glasses. I remember I was putting shooting targets on the backstop. I turned around to walk back to the shooting bench, I saw that Wayne had his pistol pointing at me. I started slowly walking toward him, a cold sensation went up my spine. I thought I was going to die, but I kept walking. Wayne put his pistol down on the bench. He said, "Satan made me do it." I replied, "Fuck you and Satan. You scared the hell out of me." My gun was on the bench next to him. I picked up my gun. I wanted to kill him and get this nightmare over. I pointed the gun at him. Messier quickly said, "Junior, the gun is not loaded. I can't make you famous if you kill me." I put the gun back on the bench. I couldn't believe that the son of a bitch unloaded my gun. He was always one step ahead of me. He was playing cat and mouse with me just like he did with the San Francisco police and the newspaper. I can't mentally take this anymore. I have to do something even if it's murder!

Finally, I became a father on November 22, 1970. Linda had a baby girl. We named the baby Pamela Ottoboni. I was very happy that day, but it did not take long for bad news to come.

Dino got very sick, and in the end of 1970, he went into the hospital. Dino had cancer and he died early in 1971. Not only do I have the problem of the "Zodiac" killer getting caught, but I'm next in line to be Chief of Police. Oh, my God! What do I do now!

One day in the spring of 1971, I was at home with my wife, Joey C. came to visit me. I noticed that he was very upset, so we went to talk in the basement. He was furious and full of hatred. He turned around and kicked my basement door, putting a hole in it. My wife was yelling from upstairs "what happened, is everything okay?"

I said "Joey put a hole in the door!" She replied, "Please leave the house." We left and I took him to my father's shooting range. I was thinking of a place where we could talk, and I could attempt to calm him down. Joey told me he was going to Los Angeles, California. He was hired to kill someone. I knew Joey had always wanted to be a hit man, so I wasn't shocked. I tried to change his mind, but Joey loved to hurt people. He was a dangerous man, ready to explode!

All of a sudden I had an idea! I knew Wayne had to die, someone had to stop him, and Joey would kill anybody. I asked Joey "When are you going to Los Angeles? Joey stated, "I don't know, but soon." I quickly replied "When you finish the job in Los Angeles, call me and give me your phone number?" Joey asked me if I was in trouble, I told him what happened in Lake Tahoe Wayne could be the Zodiac Killer! Joey smiled at me and said "Zodiac Killer, are you sure? " I replied, "I believe he is!" Joey told me to be careful and don't do anything until he gets back. When we finally left the shooting range, I felt good about myself. I hope God will forgive me. I had no other choice!

In the summer of 1971, I was Assistant Chief of Police of Colma. Wayne was not the same man I knew. Something was wrong! But I didn't know what it was. I knew he was the "Zodiac," but I had no proof.

Wayne told me he was moving to Los Angeles, California. He was going to live with a relative. He gave me a phone number and address. I was very happy, but is he going to kill someone in Los Angeles? If he gets caught, will he tell the police that I was his accomplice in Lake Tahoe? I believe he was scared because I told him my father knew who he was.

I remember the night I drove him to the airport. I was nauseous and sick to my stomach because I knew that I was letting the "Zodiac" killer getaway. I felt a cold chill all through my body, knowing that he could kill another innocent person. Oh well, it's too late now! I was getting closer to the airport when Wayne said to me, "I'll never forget you. You will be famous someday." Even today, I think of what he told me. Also, in a sorrowful tone of voice he said, "I am sorry that I involve you in Lake Tahoe. I just wanted to be like my father." **It seemed like Wayne was confessing to me. I never knew what he meant by telling me about his father.(In 2007 I found out Wayne was trying to tell me that his father also was a killer!)**

Finally, I was at the airport. I remembered all the police departments that were after him and they never caught him. I hate to say this but I "Admired him." Not for the killing he did, but because he never got caught. I always felt sorry for Wayne, it was his father's fault. Wilfred played a major part in Wayne's life. Especially in his killing spree. I don't know how the father provoked him to do what he did! But Wilfred was the catalyst. Wayne's last words to me were, "I hated pigs, but you I admired." When I saw him walk away with a suitcase, I prayed to God for forgiveness for what I had done. As I drove away I was crying like a baby. Since he stopped killing in 1970, it's been 10 months since he killed anybody. **That is the same time the "Zodiac" stopped killing.**

I kept in touch with Wayne to see if everything was okay. But In 1972, I called Wayne many times and there was no answer. That was not good! Sooner or later Wayne was going to kill again. I couldn't sleep that night, waking up sweating and dreaming about the "Zodiac" starting to kill again!

In October 1972 my father told me there was a complaint filed against me. I said, "What the hell did I do now!" My father explained to me, I was accused of letting a known criminal accompany me in my police vehicle. Also, my father stated South San Francisco, California Police department refused to let Colma Police Department monitor its radio channels. I immediately asked my father, "Who filed the complaint?" My father didn't know, but he angrily asked me, "Who was the criminal in your police vehicle? Was it Wayne?" I replied, "No, Wayne is not wanted by the police and no one knows what he did in the Lake Tahoe!" I took a deep breath and said, "It had to be Joey C. I had him in my police vehicle numerous times."

I was getting nervous because my father was getting very angry with me. I had to tell him about Joey C. I explained to him that Joey C. Killed a black kid, when he was a juvenile. My father grabbed me by the collar and heatedly asked, "Who the hell is Joey C.?" I was always scared of my father. I knew he had a violent temper. I told him I knew Joey C. A long time and I'm sorry for having him in my police vehicle. My father walked away saying, "You are the Chief of Police, don't get in any more trouble you fucken idiot!" I didn't have the nerve to tell my father that Joey C. was now a hired assassin. I knew my father was right, but I'm going to need this service of Joey C. To kill Wayne Messier!

The next month, during work hours, I was all messed up. All the time I thought of Wayne, it was driving me crazy. I didn't know if he was in jail or worse yet, did he kill anyone? There was an incident that took place during my job where I was almost killed. I was dispatched to the Colma dump, it was located off Junipero Serra Blvd. There was a complaint that someone had a pitchfork and was trying to kill somebody.

I arrived at the scene, and observed a caucasian male waving a pitchfork toward another male. I immediately proceeded out of my police vehicle. I then took out my revolver, as I was walking toward the suspect, I shouted, "drop the pitchfork or I'll kill you." After I said that the suspect was now coming toward me waving the pitchfork. I held my revolver in a tripod position, yelling, "Stop! Don't come any closer!" But something happened to me. Oh my god! I couldn't fire my revolver. Thank God. A Broadmoor police vehicle pulled up and Officer Jerry Shaffer proceeded out of his vehicle and was shouting, "Ray, you are in my line of fire!" I quickly turned to my right, and Officer Shaffer was directly in front of the suspect.

Another Broadmoor police vehicle arrived, and both Broadmoor police officers handcuffed the suspect and then they arrested him. I was so embarrassed! This was my prisoner, and I was the Chief of Police. I never wanted to be a police officer, and that proves it. I couldn't shoot that suspect. Officer Shaffer asked me what happened. I told him, "I couldn't pull the trigger." When both police officers left, I thought of Wayne Messier. The same thing happened to me at Lake Tahoe! I couldn't kill Wayne! I remembered Wayne telling me that I should never have been a cop. I will never forget what happened that day!

In December of 1972, I called up Joey C.(the hit man) now living in Los Angeles. I was scared when I told him, "I need a favor." I have to find Wayne, he moved to Los Angeles, and he isn't answering the phone. I was scared that something bad had happened to him. If I find where he is, will you kill him? I don't want to do this Joey, but I have no other choice! If he is the "Zodiac" killer, he's got to be stopped. The police are never going to capture him, so I have to do this! Joey C. in a soft tone, I barely could hear him, "Ray, I will take care of him." I yelled at him, "No, Joey! Let me go to Los Angeles and see what happened to him!" Joey replied, "Okay! We do it your way."

Call me when you are in Los Angeles. I was thankful that he was going to help me solve this nightmare. Joey isn't just a hit man; he inflicts punishment to his victims. I thought of something evil, if Joey kills Wayne, then I have to kill Joey. Oh, my God! What the hell is happening to me! I realized that God is getting even with me. Remember in 1970 I went with Wayne to the Church of Satan! Before I finished talking to Joey, I asked him, "How much do you want?" Joey said, "I don't want your money, you helped me, and now I'll help you!" After talking to Joey, I couldn't stop crying. I was emotionally Fucked-up. The only thing that came to my mind was, "Wayne has to die!"

I want you to imagine how a killer's mind functions! His name is Joey C. A national born Killer. When he was a Juvenile, he killed a black kid. He showed no mercy! I hate to say This but he is still my friend. He did something that was hideous! In the mid 1960's, a person paid Joe C. $200 to beat someone up! Not only Joey C. beat up this person, he broke his arm. The damaged arm was amputated! Three months later, this person committed suicide! Joe C. Is a dangerous man!

Chapter VI

Chief of Police

I was all alone! Broadmoor police patrolled Colma on the nights and weekends. I was inexperience about police work. The police academy expects rookie cops to learn police work from their department. Colma was a unique police department. Broadmoor police wanted to take over the Colma Police Department! They wanted me to quit!

I went to see Capt. William Cann, of the San Bruno Police Department, (San Bruno is south of San Francisco) I met him at a police banquet in 1970. He was a gentleman and I felt comfortable talking to him. He already knew of me because he read about me in the newspaper. I was Assistant Chief of Police and I needed help! I asked Capt. Cann if I could ride with a police officer at night to get more knowledge about police work. He stated "Yes, you can, but you would have to sign a paper releasing the San Bruno Police Department of any liabilities. Capt. Cann helped me tremendously, if it were not for him, I would have been in trouble!

I knew there was a lot of pressure on the Town Council to appoint a Chief of Police. My father and my cousin were on the Town Council. I knew my father wanted me to be the Chief of Police. So, I already knew I was going to be the next Chief of Police. My life would be awful if I became Chief of Police. I didn't want to be Chief of Police, it was my father's idea and he was the boss!

Police Department, newspapers and my father's enemies, of which there were many, will be watching me day and night! There were about 25 applications for the job of Chief of Police. There were policemen, ex-policeman and Chiefs of Police, all applying for the job. Everyone had more experience and knowledge than me. In December of 1971, I was appointed Chief of Police. That was the start of my downfall. From then on my life became a living hell!

There was one day I will never forget! When I became Chief of Police, I had 5 reserve officers. It was on a Monday afternoon, I went to visit one of my reserve officers at the local hospital. His name was Mike Fields. He was dying of cancer. There was no hope. He was only 21 years old. It was 38 years ago and I never forgot what he told me. In a sad voice, he said "why is this happening to me? I did nothing wrong to deserve this." When I left I was crying like a baby. I immediately went to my church and lit a candle for him. He died one month later.

Let me get back to when I was Chief of Police. Don't get me wrong, it was a great honor to be Chief of Police. The name "Ottoboni" was one of the most respectable names in San Mateo County. I couldn't at any time disgrace the family name! I was involved with a serial killer. I was a compulsive gambler. There was no way I could keep the family name from being disgraced. Besides that, I hate this **Fucking Job**!

There was one thing I enjoyed about being Chief of Police. They were filming the streets of San Francisco, the famous television series. They had to get permission from the Chief of Police. That was no problem. I was watching while they were filming the scenes and I had the distinguished pleasure of meeting Karl Malden, the great character actor. Mr. Malden came over to me, introduced himself and asked me if I would join him for lunch? Naturally, I said yes. We had lunch at the Cypress Hills restaurant. It is located off Hillside Boulevard in Colma, California. The restaurant is very close to my father's shooting range.

I enjoyed talking with Mr. Malden, he was an exciting person. Mr. Malden shocked me when he told me he didn't like acting! I didn't know what to say. He won and an Academy award as a supporting actor in "On the Waterfront" I saw Karl Malden in many movies. He was a great actor! He mentioned to me that he was married for a long time. I remember he asked me "If I liked my job?" I told him "No I don't!" Mr. Malden asked me, "Why do you hate your job." I replied, "My job is all politics and I hate politics!" He never said a word, just smiled and shook his head. Meeting Mr. Malden made my day!

In January of 1972, after one month of being Chief of Police something unusual happened. I was on patrol on El Camino Real. I observed a motorcycle speeding southbound. I never had time to get a reading on my radar. Because I was listening to a baseball game on my transistor radio, I made the traffic stop in South San Francisco. The dispatcher asked me if I needed assistance. I said "No I don't!"

I approached the driver of the motorcycle and identified the driver as a Hells Angel. I asked him for his driver's license. I immediately went back to my vehicle to see if the driver had any warrants. He had none. I was in a good mood, because I was winning the game on my transistor radio. I gave him back his driver's license and I told him, "I never want to see you speeding in my city again! He thanked me and said "You are the policeman that's been in the newspaper. You were Councilman, Mayor and now Chief of Police. You are the hero of the Hells Angels motorcycle gang! I didn't know what to say. Finally, I said "you got to be kidding me." The motorcycle driver replied "Will you come to one of our meetings, or am I insulting you?" I replied "no you're not insulting me; I would like to attended a Hells Angel meeting." He gave me the address in San Francisco.

The meeting was on a Wednesday night at 8 o'clock. I arrived at the meeting, I was late about 15 minutes and I was scared! As I walked into the meeting they all knew I wasn't a Hells Angel. When the speaker announced who I was they were all clapping. I was feeling uneasy. They gave me a warm welcome; also they made me a **member** of the **Hells Angels!**

Three months later, I found out what police work was all about. I was parked southbound on El Camino Real, watching for speeders and suddenly, over my police radio the dispatcher from South San Francisco's stated that a bank was robbed and the suspect's vehicle was then heading my way. I remember saying **Oh Fuck!** I observed the vehicle coming northbound onto El Camino Real. I knew I was in trouble. The suspect's vehicle was going very fast and approximately 8 police vehicles was following in the rear. I didn't have time to think about the situation. I immediately got in position behind the suspect's vehicle, then I observed one of the suspects shooting at my police vehicle then I made a **foolish mistake**. I got in the middle between the suspect's vehicle and the police vehicles. Then I got in the right lane and I was scared! The suspect was shooting at my vehicle and I knew I couldn't shoot back. A **bullet** hit my **front bumper**. I pulled over to the shoulder of the road, to let the other police officers go ahead of me. That was 38 years ago, but I remember saying "**what the Fuck am I doing**

here!" The suspect's vehicle was apprehended in Daly City, California. One suspect was killed, and the other was arrested.

That night, I told my father I didn't want to be a policeman anymore. My father didn't listen to a word I said.

The media, police departments and my father's enemies were waiting for me to fail as Chief of Police. There was so much pressure on me, and some nights I couldn't sleep. Every month, that I was chief of police, became more difficult for me to perform my duties.

Later in 1972, something happened to me, that I had absolutely no control of! I have no idea how these people knew of me!

Chapter VII

The Mob

The first contact I had with the mob was in the summer of 1972. The mob, back then isn't like it is today. They will approach you personally and if you don't cooperate with them they would harm your family! Today it is different. They will never approach you! Someone else will. Anyway, let me tell you what happened to me in 1972!

I was driving northbound on Junipero Serra Boulevard in my police vehicle, when a driver of a black limousine signaled me to pull over off the roadway.(That was a dirt road next to the Colma Dump.) Immediately, I got out of my vehicle and approached the limousine. (Those days the only radio we had was a walkie-talkie.) The driver in the limousine told me "Will you please get in the back of the limousine!" In a different situation I would have never got in that car. I knew I had no other choice. Remember I'm all by myself. I had no backup! And no radio! This is amazing I wasn't scared, if they wanted to kill me, they would already have done it! I got in the back seat of the limousine. There were two men wearing suits. The one who did the talking was polite. This is bizarre! All the time I was in the limousine, they never disarmed me! I kept my composure! He wanted to rent three houses in Colma, they must have known my father owned many houses in Colma. They would pay my bookie $10,000, also they would pay rent of $5000 per month.

I was shocked that they knew I owed $10,000, I didn't know what to say! I was getting nervous, but I had enough sense to keep my mouth shut! They told me someone would contact me. They advised me the conversation, which took place in the limousine, never happened. I wanted to tell someone but I knew that would be dangerous. I could have told my father, he had powerful friends. But I didn't, no matter how powerful you are the mob will kill you!

The mob was in Colma for three years. My job was to keep Broadmoor police away from the street. 408, 410 and 412 E. St. was in an alley! You had to pass through an unlocked gate to get to those houses! There was a narrow passage way between the houses! E St. was a dead end street. It was a perfect set up.

I didn't want to be involved with gangsters, but there was nothing I could do to **escape them**! My family was in danger, including my powerful father. What was I supposed to do? I was scared; they would kill my wife and daughter! All the time, my parents never knew about my **involvement with the mob**!

I kept a close watch on the three houses on E street. I was living at 421 F St. It was about 100 feet away from those houses. I made sure there wasn't a Broadmoor police vehicle on that street! Remember I was Chief of Police, Broadmoor police couldn't do any surveillance in my area. Especially, in one of my houses. Before they do any surveillance they must contact me. Now you know why the mob never got caught!

The mob contacted me, wanting to talk to me. I was scared because I knew they wanted something from me. They sent two of their gangsters to my house to pick me up. They patted me down and let me in the car and took me to San Francisco. There were two of them, I could tell they were carrying guns. They didn't blindfold me because they knew I wouldn't talk because my family was in danger. When we got to the house it was pitch black outside.

The garage door opened and we went into the garage. When the garage started to close I knew I might not see my family again. I wanted to cry but I couldn't! The driver got out of the car followed by the man in the back with me, then I got out. We walked into the house and I saw a person on the couch that I had never seen before. I walked in and stood before him waiting for him to speak. He got right to the point but was very demanding. He told me they needed to rent more houses. I was startled and in a soft voice I told him I couldn't rent him anymore houses. I said to him, the more houses you have the bigger chance for you to get caught. He replied how is that little girl of yours. I got real scared and realized I really have no choice in the matter. I asked him how many houses do you need? He replied three more houses.

I remembered the three very small houses in the alley, they were for 415 A-B-C on F Street. I told the man the houses were very small, would that be a problem? He said no, as long as you do your job keeping the cops away. He then stated they would pay me $3000 more per month. I agreed to that and told him I would do everything in my power to keep the cops away. After that statement, I slowly walked away. He then stated remember you have a daughter, I hope you don't disappoint me. On the way home in my mind I knew I had no other choice but to cooperate with them.

It was very difficult for me to perform my job as chief of police, when I knew I was committing a crime!

Many time I wanted to quit my job. Also I was going to inform Broadmoor Police, that six houses were being used for drug trafficking! Everyday, I thought of doing that, but the consequence would be fatal to my family! I didn't know what to do, so I did nothing! Can you imagine, if I contacted Broadmoor Police, what do you think would have happened? I would have been arrested for giving shelter to criminals, also being involved in a conspiracy to commit a crime? No matter what I do, right or wrong, I am totally, fucked! For three years, I went through this fucken nightmare. Thank GOD, my parents didn't know what I was doing!

I knew all the time those six houses that belonged to my parents were used for drug trafficking! I'm not proud of what I did. All the time I was involved with the mob, I had absolutely no choice. I knew I was Chief of Police, and what I did was against the law. My family was in danger, so I believe I made the right decision.

Now maybe I'm wrong, but put yourself in my situation! **To the reader**, what would you have done? Was I a bad cop? I don't believe I was. When you don't have control of the situation and your family is in danger! I don't believe I am responsible for what I did. That is why I'm still alive! I believe **you the reader** would agree with me.

In 1974 when I resigned as chief of police, the mob Left Colma! I never knew any names, so I was no threat to them.

Chapter VIII

Nightmares

(1973 – 1974)

In January of 1973, an FBI agent(His name I don't remember) came to see me at my police station. I was shocked to see him. I knew he was a friend of my father! He was one of the highest ranked agents in the FBI office in San Francisco, California. He said my father informed him of my involvement in Lake Tahoe, also he said "Where is Wayne?" I replied, "He is in Los Angeles, California. I don't know if he is alive or dead. I know he is not in jail, because it would have been in the newspaper!" The FBI agent replied "are you sure he is the "Zodiac" killer?" I said "No, I'm not positive, but after he left Los Angeles, the "Zodiac" killings stopped. I'm going to Los Angeles. If Wayne is alive, I have someone that will kill him. Please don't stop me!" The agent slowly backed away from me and said "You are crazy; you are going to get caught. This conversation never took place." I replied " Wayne is going to kill again." The FBI agent walked away, angry and very depressed.

In 1973 my wife was expecting a baby in May. So, I should be happy, but I'm not. Terrible events were coming my way. I had to go to Los Angeles, California to find out if the "Zodiac" killer is still alive. I boarded the airplane; I have a horrible fear of flying. When I got off the airplane, I was all Fucked-up and I wanted to go back and I almost did. I pushed myself to go on. The most frightening thought that came to me was where is Wayne? Hopefully, he's not in jail. I was going to rent a car, but decided taking a cab would be the easiest way to go.

I took a cab to the address that Wayne gave me. When I got there I told the cab driver to wait. I knocked on the door and a woman answered. I asked her if she knows where Wayne Messier is. She replied, "Who are you?" I told her I'm a police officer and a friend of Wayne's. She stared at me with her eyes wide open, and slowly said, "Wayne is dead." I was shocked and happy at the same time. I replied, "When did he die?" She said, "Wayne died in December of last year (1972)." I replied, "Where is he buried?" She didn't answer me. She looked frightened. I believe she was a relative, could've been Wayne's mother. Then I got back in a cab and went to the Los Angeles courthouse. Again I told the cab driver to wait. He asked me, "Whom are you looking for?" I replied, "I'm a police officer, and I was looking for a serial killer and I found him." The cab drivers stated, "where is he?" In a sad voice I said, "Thank God, he is finally dead." The cab driver asked, "What was that serial killers name?" I smiled and said, "I can't reveal his name to you and if I did ,you wouldn't believe me anyway."

After I left the cab, I went to look up Wayne Messier's death certificate. It is located in the vital statistics records. I found out that Wayne Messier died in Los Angeles on December 11, 1972, and was shipped to Sacramento, California, the next day. How come Wayne's father, Wilfred, wanted his son buried as quickly as possible? Wayne was buried in Mount Vernon Cemetery in Fair Oaks, California, that's next to Sacramento, California.

I took the cab back to the airport. During the plane ride back to San Francisco, the idea went through my mind over and over, "no one will ever know who the "Zodiac" was!" Who is going to believe me! I have to tell about what happened to the "Zodiac", no matter what happens to me. I owe it to Donna Lass and the memories of other victims of "Zodiac". I was happy and relieved that Wayne was dead because the "Zodiac" killings would stop. I didn't want to go to the cemetery, but I had to.

When I got back to Colma, I called up Joey C. and told him "Zodiac" is dead. Joey C. replied, "I'm happy for you." The next day I had to tell my father the good news. I was so happy when I told him the "Zodiac" was dead! My father was a vicious man, and couldn't tolerate failure. He has never forgiven me for my involvement in the murder in Lake Tahoe. I don't think my father ever believed Wayne was the "Zodiac" killer, and I couldn't prove Wayne was the "Zodiac" killer!

Three days later I went to the Mount Vernon Cemetery in Fair Oaks, California. I stood over his tombstone and I said, "Someday I'll be back to let everybody know who you are! Finally, "Zodiac" is dead."

Later in 1973, my father approached me and stated "Someone is blackmailing me" he was angry and violent when he asked me if I had told anyone about Lake Tahoe. I replied "I told Capt. Cann, who is now Chief of Police of Union City, California. He isn't going to tell anyone! My father was yelling at me saying "You stupid son of a bitch." I knew my father had powerful friends. (Like Joe Alioto, Mayor of San Francisco)

Two months later, Joe Alioto came to Colma Police Station to see me. He stated to me "Keep your mouth shut, everything will be okay!" I was scared that Mayor Alioto knew that I was involved with the "Zodiac" in 1970! I also was afraid that something might happen to Capt. Cann.

In 1974, I read in the San Francisco Examiner newspaper that Chief Cann was assassinated by a sniper. I firmly believe that Chief Cann was innocent of any crime,or conspiracy involving the blackmailing of my father. I have never met a nicer person than William Cann. Union City Police Department arrested Leonard Baca for the murder of Chief William Cann. If Leonard Baca didn't work for **the mob,** which I don't know, the Union City Police Department had the wrong man. Capt. Cann was killed by the **mob.**The Union City Police Department was under an extreme amount of pressure to close the case on William Cann!

All the time I was a policeman, I escorted many motorist to the grave of Wyatt Earp, the famous Marshall of Dodge City, Kansas, in the late 1800's. He died in Los Angeles, California, in 1929. When his wife died in 1944, they were both buried in Colma, California. Many tourists drove to Colma just to take a picture of the grave of Wyatt Earp. That was the only thing I liked about my job!

Chapter Ix

Fired

(1974 – 1975)

In 1974, I told my father "**I wanted to quit**! I cannot take this fucken job anymore." My father didn't want me to quit, but he knew all the **mental pain** and **suffering** I went through.

One month later, **I resigned** as Chief of Police, but I stayed on as a patrolman. That was my **biggest mistake**! The newspaper stated I was asked to resign. **That's a lie!** No one told me to **resign.** That was my **decision.**

The new Chief of Police made my life a **living hell**! I worked nights and hated it. My life as a patrolman in Colma became worse. The police from neighboring cities were laughing at me. I couldn't believe so many policemen, some of which I have never met, were so happy. I found out later, those policemen were happy because I wasn't Chief of Police anymore. I hated policemen. They are hypocrites! Broadmoor policeman were happy, they were always jealous of me. That is amazing I always treated them with respect! The **Broadmoor police** can go **fuck themselves.**

I complained to my father, the chief of police is driving me crazy. He wants me to quit. I believe he was hired to fire me. Also I told my father let me quit before he fires me. Obviously, my father disagreed with me. This time I know my father was wrong. I knew my days as a policeman were numbered, but somebody is going to pay for this.

I got fired in 1975. I was set up! The Chief of Police and some members of the town Council were involved. This was a conspiracy! The accusations against me were, I was drunk off-duty and harassing a female! I never drank any alcohol in my life! The town Council wanted me out of the police force. My father was helpless. Actually, they did me a favor! I was a policeman for six years and every day was a living hell. That night at the town Council meeting, "I told them I will be back." One of the Councilman stated "is that a threat?" I replied as I am walking away, "no that's a promise."

The next day I turned in my badge and identification to the Chief of Police. I told him "you set me up" and "I will get even!" he replied "I know my days are numbered!"

One month later, I found out the female who was a deputy sheriff, was a friend of the chief of police. **It was a perfect set up!**

In a large city, when a policeman gets fired, it's not important! The newspaper doesn't care, the media doesn't know about it! In a small town like Colma, when a policeman gets fired it is a major ordeal. Especially, when your name is Ray Ottoboni. In Colma history, I was the only policeman ever to get fired.

In 1964 and 1968, I made headlines as being the youngest councilman and the youngest mayor in California. When you're on top you are a target for the newspaper. After I got fired, I didn't know where to go. In a small town there is nowhere to hide!

During the end of 1975 after I knew I was framed, I wanted revenge I was thinking of running for councilman in the 1976 elections. Somehow I had to get even with my enemies and I knew who they were! I was very religious, so I tried to erase my thoughts of getting even. But in politics, that is impossible! Naturally, my name was in three newspapers, telling the media that I got fired.

.

Colma, Is a small town, the local news travels very fast? I had to get my dignity back, especially when I did nothing wrong. My father was happy; I was going to run again in the next election. I filed my nomination papers as a candidate in the 1976 election.

Linda left me in 1975. She couldn't deal with the threatening phone calls and my major gambling problem. She took the children and went to live with her parents in Redwood City, California.

Chapter X

Arrested

(1976 – 1979)

1976, was another year I wanted to forget. The "Zodiac" killer is dead. Donna Lass will never be found and Chief William Cann was assassinated!

You the reader, this year is the worst year of my life. I hope I don't lose my sanity!

I was leaving my house on F street in Colma, when I got arrested by two Deputy Sheriff officers. Naturally, Colma police was assisting them! They must have loved that. I was in shock; I didn't know why they were arresting me. A Deputy Sheriff Officer read me my rights. When I was arrested, my father also was arrested at his house. My mother was handcuffed and then an officer said "Let her go!" Me and my father were locked up in jail at Daly City, California. The police let my father go immediately, they only wanted me. I was released on bail. I left the jail very depressed. I was saying to myself "I got framed." The Chief of Police succeeded in his plan to get rid of me!

When I got home, my father told me everything that had happened. The police forced him to open his gun room. My father was a big gun collector of many guns, rifles and shotguns. There was a FBI agent with the local police. The agent asked my father "where is the Thomson Submachine gun." My father replied, "I don't have a submachine gun!" The FBI agent said "yes, you do and we are going to find it." My father told me the agent was standing on top of the trap door, that is where the submachine gun was hidden.(**Isn't that unbelievable**) My father was frightened, but kept his composure. The police searched the gun room, but couldn't find the submachine gun.

The next day, my father who got the submachine gun from Dino, the Chief of Police , buried it. My father never told me where he buried the machine gun.

The following week my father hired two lawyers. They cost him a lot of money. The lawyers told me the District Attorney is making sure he is going to win, because it's the first time, in San Mateo County, that's a candidate ever got arrested for Vote Fraud. Oh, my God! **I am totally fucked**!

After I got arrested, I knew I had no chance of winning the town election. I got arrested one month before the election**.**

You the reader, what does that tell you? Was I set up? Yes I was! Everything is **crooked** even the **police.**

I wasn't the same person. Naturally it was in the newspapers that I got arrested. I lost the election by **one vote**! Yes, I said one vote! That's how powerful the Ottoboni name is. There was a conspiracy against me.

The District Attorney charged me with 15 felony counts, of vote fraud. I was charged with illegally listing voters in homes owned by my father, supposedly to vote for me. Now that is a lie. That is ridiculous! **You the reader**, when a person gets in a voting booth, that person can vote for any candidate and no one will ever know**. Do you agree with me? Anyway keep reading!**

The District Attorney, In 1976 was a **fucking liar**! He hated my father, so I don't have to say anymore. The Deputy Sheriff officers twisted and turned everything I said in their favor. I had no other choice, but to plead no contest, which is a guilty plea. My political career was over and the family name was disgraced.

I didn't go to trial. The judge reduced all the felonies to misdemeanors, also the judge placed me on probation for three years. I have to do 600 hours of public service. I had to promise the judge, that I would never go back to politics.

Where do I go now, in a small town, there is nowhere you can hide!

Everyone turned against me, even my friends! Remember, everybody knew I was guilty, but I wasn't! My father was deeply hurt by me getting arrested. I thought he would never forgive me. He would never talk to me it was awful, I felt like a outcast! I went to church many times, praying to "GOD".

I needed his help and most of the time, it made me feel good. I always believed in revenge, which was against my religious belief. I couldn't forget that I was framed! Someone is going to pay for this! I don't know how or where, if this doesn't happen, I can't live with myself!

After doing the public service and my probation was completed I was a free man.(Many years later, I got an attorney to clear my record. Two months later, my record was cleared. This means the vote fraud conviction never happened.)

I thought it was bad when I got arrested. Well, it's twice as bad now. I could not tell anyone that I was not guilty. So all the people of **Colma**, the **newspapers** and the **media** knows I was guilty of vote fraud. But I was **not guilty**. I did nothing wrong.

I want **the reader**, to know no matter if a person gives money to someone or threatens someone to vote for that person, When the voter goes into voting booth, no one knows who the person voted for. There is no way to know! So what the hell was I guilty of?

The District Attorney said that I gave free rent if they voted for me. The undercover cops stated I said they wouldn't have to pay rent, so they can vote for me. Again I am saying how will I know that they voted for me? That is totally bullshit!

To the reader, I know what really happened. Cops are just like criminals, they lie and they make you say things you don't mean. Do you believe me? I hope so, there's no reason for me to lie to you!

I hate to talk bad about cops. They are not all bad, but in certain situations when they are ordered to arrest someone. The police will do everything in their power to incarcerate that person. Even if it's legal or illegal. Right or wrong, that's the way the system works!

To the reader, you knew I was **framed!** Keep reading this book. Let's see if the District Attorney actually won the case against me. You will know the answer in the next chapter. **Just be patient, keep reading!**

As the years go by, I realized that I was not the same person. I have changed so much, I don't know myself anymore. I pray to "God" for help. I went to church asked "God" to forgive me. I believed I was punished by "God" for what I did in Lake Tahoe. In my heart I knew "God" forgave me for what happened to Donna Lass. Only "God" knows I was innocent of any knowledge that Donna Lass was going to be murdered.

After I got arrested, the next three years were terrible! I hated myself because all the pain I caused my parents. I hated people. No one would speak to me, because I got arrested. How quickly, people forget if it wasn't for me and my father, Daly City, California would have taken control of Colma. When you are in power, they are your friends. When you lose that power, they don't even know your name.

In 1979, an event took place, I can't explain how this happened, or why this happened!

You the reader, this will **shock you**. I promise, you will not believe me, but I can prove this event took place. **Are you ready**!

My parents purchased a new 1979 Ford Thunderbird for me at a dealership in South San Francisco, California. I knew Bob Lopez, part owner of the company. He was also my bookmaker. I was unemployed, so my parents paid cash for the vehicle. I had the vehicle for three months. One day I drove my vehicle to the dealership, to get it serviced. When I got there, Bob was there and he was very angry. I owned him $10,000. I told him I will get the money from my parents, but I need more time. Bob was furious and I knew why. He needed the money now. He was responsible for the money because he is the middle man. I knew it would take approximately an hour to service my vehicle, so I read a book in the waiting room.

A half-hour later Bob told me to come to his office. I knew Bob a long time and he hasn't changed. He was always a snappy dresser. He was sitting down behind his desk, staring at me. I immediately asked him is there something wrong? He said ,"they took your vehicle." I replied, in an angry tone, what are you talking about, where is my vehicle?" Bob said "two men took your vehicle because you own them $10,000. I totally lost it. I was yelling at Bob, "I cannot believe you let that happen. If I go home without that vehicle you are a dead man, you **Fucken Idiot**!" Bob replied, I have no control of what happened. Ray, you know I always told you, "If you win, you get paid. If you lose, you pay. Do you fucken understand?" I didn't know what to do I was so scared. I asked Bob "I need a ride home". When we got to Colma, as I got out of his car, I told him "my father is a powerful man and also he is crazy." The gun you have in your office, you are going to need it. He just laughed at me, and said "I'm not scared."

When I got home and told my mother what happened, she broke down in tears. I knew my mother was going to tell my father, so all I could do is wait. When my father approached me he was enraged. He slapped me in the face and told me to get in the fucken truck. On the way to the dealership, he didn't say a word to me. I was scared to death. Especially, when I saw a 45 automatic pistol in a holster lying on the front seat of his truck. I pleaded with my father to go back . I promised him I would get the car back. My father told me "to shut up." I was so scared, he was going to kill Bob. When we got to the dealership, my father parked the truck on the street next to the dealership .

Before he got out of the car he asked me what is the fuckers name. I replied "Bob Lopez." He immediately took the gun out of the holster, and put it under his coat. I yelled at him, "be careful, Bob has a gun underneath his desk on his right side." Bob had a 22 revolver in his office desk. I wasn't worried about my father getting shot. Bob had no chance against my father, but I was scared of my father getting into trouble for having a pistol in a public place. I got out of the truck to see if I could stop this, before someone got killed. I saw my father coming out of the building and then I knew no one got shot. Thank God! My father got back in the truck and then I started to get in the passenger side. My father told me, "walk home you bum." When he drove away, I was talking to myself, how could this happen. My poor parents, I am putting them through hell. I went back in the building to talk to Bob; if I had a gun I would've killed him. When I went in his office I looked at him and said "you are a lucky man, my father is involved with the mob." Bob replied very angry, "is he going to have me killed?" I replied, I don't know and I don't care. Take me home you mother fucker. Bob gave me a ride home, he felt bad about what he did! **I never saw that car again!**

During that time, the Ford Thunderbird was the best car I ever had. Today, 31 years ago when I think of that terrible day, I still don't believe that happened. Unfortunately, it did!

Three months later, my parents got me another new car, but this time the car was registered under my father's name. I wonder why, my father did that! My parents paid my gambling debts for many years. They gave me' $500,000, before they died. I gave my parents a lot of pain and suffering!

To the reader, after all the misery I caused my father I thought my father was going to have me killed! I told my mother I was afraid of what might happen to me. After my involvement with the "Zodiac" killer and then I got arrested in 1976 and now I lost the new car that he bought me. I told my mother I believe my father had enough agony from me. Mom, you know my father is involved with the mob. Do you think he would have me killed? My mother replied your father loves you, he would never do that!

Later that year, I had terrifying dreams almost every week. I used to wake up many nights sweating. It was an **angel** from "God" telling me to run in the 1980 election, or was it **destiny!**

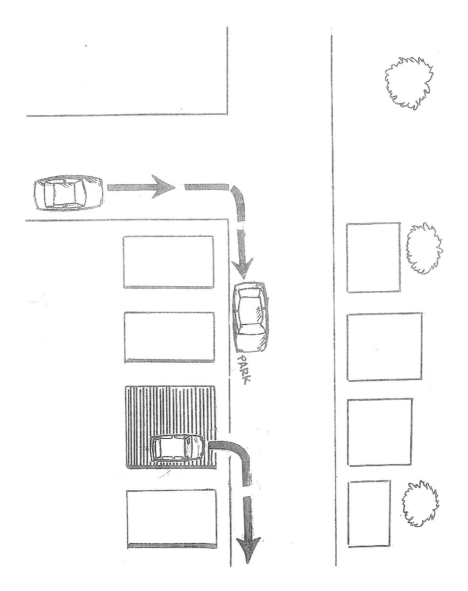

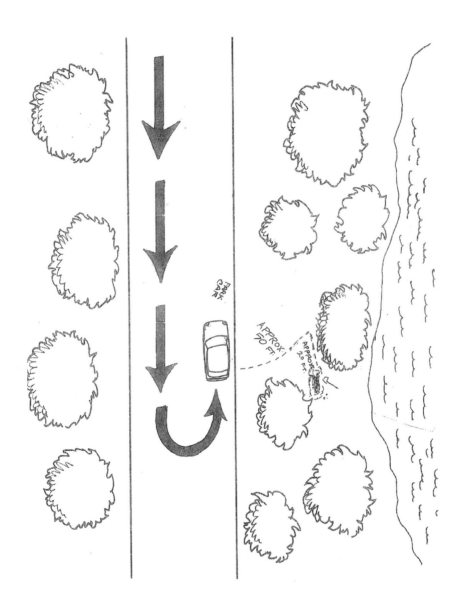

REWARD
$10,000.00

∃PTWYPNWA□▲W⊁SN2⅂
△△Q∙∙∙∙∙■▲ZZW⅄W□□∙

Last seen caring for a patient at the Sahara Tahoe Casino First Aid Station

Donna Lass, RN

Missing since 1:30am on September 6th, 1970

Family and investigators have made great progress in this case. We are confident that her abductor/murderer will be arrested, tried and found guilty. If you have any further information that can help us finalize our investigation, that will locate Donna and/or result in a successful prosecution; please contact the South Lake Tahoe Police Department
530 542-6100

Colma political leaders arrested for voter fraud

By STEVE NASH
Staff writer

Two Colma leaders were under arrest Tuesday on felony charges of voter fraud brought in a county Grand Jury indictment.

Raymond Ottoboni, Sr., 71, and his son Ray Jr., 34, who between them have held most of the official titles in tiny Colma at one time or another in past years, are accused of attempting to register non-residents to vote in the coming election.

Ottoboni. Sr., a Colma councilman for the past 25 years, and his wife Mae were released on their own recognizance after booking in Daly City on charges of voting fraud and conspiracy to commit voting fraud, a felony.

Ray Jr., a candidate in the March 2 council elections and a former councilman, mayor, police chief and police officer, was released after posting $5,000 bond.

The three are accused of inducing at least four non-residents to register to vote in Colma, using a vacant apartment at 408 E St., owned by the Ottobonis as a false address.

Ray Jr., also a deputy registrar, prepared registration affidavits for Patricia L. Clifton, Andy Morris, David Lemesh, and Arthur Ray, dated January 30.

The four were allegedly charged no rent, were told to visit the E. St. premises often enough to give the appearance of living there, and there was an understanding that they would vote for Ray Jr. in the coming election, according to District Attorney Keith Sorenson.

Details of the case are hazy and will remain so until transcripts of the Grand Jury proceedings are unsealed in ten days. But investigation is continuing and more arrests may follow, Sorenson said.

It is known that "Patricia Clifton" and "Andy Morris" are assumed names, however, leading some to believe that Ottoboni Jr. may have registered an undercover police agent or two to the E. St. address.

Sorenson confirmed that his investigators had been watching the situation since last May, when they were tipped off that such violations might occur.

Ottoboni Sr. reportedly charged after his release that his arrest was somehow connected to the March election, less than three weeks away.

"We allege that Ottoboni Jr. arranged with the four individuals to appear to live in Colma ..., and they didn't actually have to move in. This was in order to get people into Colma to vote for him ...," said Sorenson.

"The four signed a lease for the house that was supposed to last until the election, and then terminate. The two seniors aided and assisted, and all are charged with conspiracy as well," he said.

The town has only about 200 registered voters, making each vote potentially crucial. Seven candidates are running for three seats in March.

Ottoboni's Jr.'s statement of qualifications, to be mailed to Colma voters, along with a sample ballot, states in part:

"... I have done nothing I'm ashamed of. I'm proud of my accomplishments. I am running because of the apparent lack of integrity and leadership by some council members."

Ottoboni Jr. served as Colma's mayor in 1968. Later a police patrolman, he was appointed police chief by the council, headed at the time by his father.

Ray Jr. was subsequently demoted to patrolman again after he was accused of letting a known criminal acompany him in his police car.

South San Francisco police reportedly refused to let Colma monitor its radio channels at the time.

Last September the new police chief, James Dorris, fired Ottoboni Jr. after complaints from other jurisdictions about his performance.

Arraignment is scheduled for February 23.

Ray Ottoboni, Sr.

Ray Ottoboni, Jr.

Jail sentence delayed for ex-chief

A 90-day jail sentence of Colma's former police chief has been delayed for three weeks by a San Mateo County Superior Court judge and the jail time may be dropped altogether.

The stay came after a one-hour hearing Friday into the mental and nervous state of Raymond John Ottoboni, former police chief and city council member in Colma.

Ottoboni, 34, pleaded guilty in July to a charge he interfered with the election process by tampering with the registration of voters in a recall election in Colma.

Judge Frank Piombo on Aug. 21 sentenced Ottoboni to three years probation and 90 days in the county jail. Ottoboni's father, Raymond Dominic Ottoboni, 71, also pleaded guilty to a similar charge and was sentenced to two years probation and ordered to serve 50 hours of uncompensated public service.

The public service work later was dropped by Piombo. Now the judge has taken under three week's advisement the question of dropping the younger Ottoboni's term.

The hearing was called for by attorney Zerne Haning just before the former chief was due to start his jail term.

The hearing included testimony from Ottoboni's personal psychiatrist that a jail term would result in Ottoboni's hospitalization.

When Piombo and Assistant Dist. Atty. Stanley Poling suggested the possibility of some work furlough or public service alternative, Ottoboni's doctor, Dr. Allan Levy said the former official was unemployable.

Dr. Levy said he has been treating Ottoboni since July for extreme anxiety and depression.

He described Ottoboni as susceptible to ulcers and extremely nervous about the future of his criminal proceedings. Added to Ottoboni's anxiety, the doctor said, is a recent heart operation on his father and the prospect within the next month of a similar operation for his mother.

He said a jail term for Ottoboni, "would be most likely extremely deleterious and aggravate his nervous condition." Confinement, Levy said, "would lead to hospitalization for either physical or psychiatric conditions."

Ottoboni family indicted

Three members of a Colma family prominent for years in local politics have been indicted by the San Mateo County Grand Jury on an assortment of felony and misdemeanor charges involving a scheme to illegally register voters for an upcoming city council election.

One of the indicted men is a Colma town councilman. His son is a former mayor and police chief, and presently a deputy registrar of voters for the county and a candidate for councilman in the March election.

Named in the indictment are Raymond D. Ottoboni, 70, his wife, Mae, 69, and their son, Raymond Ottoboni Jr., 34. They were arrested yesterday.

The elder Ottoboni is a member of the Colma town council. His son was demoted from police chief to patrolman a year ago.

In the indictment handed down Monday night, the family is charged with procuring four persons living outside Colma to register as voters under a false Colma address.

Raymond Ottoboni top vote-getter in Colma election

Raymond Ottoboni

Veteran Colma mayor Ray Ottoboni is dead

COLMA — Raymond D. Ottoboni, who spent more than 33 years on the Colma Town Council before stepping down last December because of failing health, died Tuesday at a local convalescent hospital. He was 79.

Ottoboni was a Colma native and descendent of one of the first families to settle in the North County area. The family remains one of the largest residential property holders in Colma.

Ottoboni ran a nursery for many years and became one of the most influential residents of the small cemetery town.

He was a veritable fixture in Colma politics for most of his adult life. First elected to the council in 1950, he won re-election to eight consecutive terms, the last time in 1982.

He also served eight one-year terms as the town's mayor, sev-

See OTTOBONI, Page A8

Raymond D. Ottoboni

"Here's a superb portrait of the surreal fiction that exists in our present-day reality." — AUGUST COPPOLA

"The most striking of S.F. State's crème de la crème."
JOHN STANLEY, S.F. Chronicle

"... intriguing ..." HOWARD ROSENBERG, KOH Radio

GOLDEN GATE AWARD
SAN FRANCISCO INTERNATIONAL FILM FESTIVAL

SILVER APPLE
NATIONAL EDUCATIONAL FILM FESTIVAL

RAY OTTOBONI ... "The King of Colma"

"This is Colma, a suburb whose population of more than 1 million makes it the second largest place in California. Only 500 of them, however, are alive." — L.A. TIMES

The KING of COLMA
A BARRY BRANN FILM

213·553·8900
10250 SANTA MONICA BOULEVARD
CENTURY CITY SHOPPING CENTER

October 20-26, 1989

PRODUCED & DIRECTED by BARRY BRANN • P.O. Box 282044, San Francisco, CA 94128 • (415) 387-7322

STATE OF CALIFORNIA
CERTIFICATION OF VITAL RECORD

COUNTY OF LOS ANGELES • REGISTRAR-RECORDER/COUNTY CLERK

CERTIFICATE OF DEATH
STATE OF CALIFORNIA—DEPARTMENT OF PUBLIC HEALTH

State File Number: 7097-050109

DECEDENT PERSONAL DATA

- 1a. Name of Deceased—First Name: WAYNE
- 1b. Middle Name: T.
- 1c. Last Name: MESSIER
- 2a. Date of Death: December 11, 1972
- 2b. Hour: 6:15 A.
- 3. Sex: Male
- 4. Color or Race: White
- 5. Birthplace: California
- 6. Date of Birth: December 29, 1941
- 7. Age: 30 Years
- 8. Name and Birthplace of Father: Wilfred Messier — North Dakota
- 9. Maiden Name and Birthplace of Mother: Helen Stewart — Texas
- 10. Citizen of what Country: USA
- 11. Social Security Number: 566-56-9246
- 12. Married, Never Married, Widowed, Divorced: Married
- 13. Name of Surviving Spouse: Elaine Klotchman
- 14. Last Occupation: Engineer
- 15. Number of Years in this Occupation: 9
- 16. Name of Last Employing Company or Firm: California Highway Dep't
- 17. Kind of Industry or Business: State Government

PLACE OF DEATH

- 18a. Place of Death—Name of Hospital or Other In-Patient Facility: Memorial Hospital of Glendale
- 18b. Street Address: 1420 So. Central Ave.
- 18c. Inside City Corporate Limits: Yes
- 18d. City or Town: Glendale
- 18e. County: Los Angeles
- 18f. Length of Stay in County of Death: 9 Years
- 18g. Length of Stay in California: Life

USUAL RESIDENCE

- 19a. Usual Residence—Street Address: 4061 Rhodes Ave.
- 19b. Inside City Corporate Limits: Yes
- 20. Name and Mailing Address of Informant: Elaine Ruth Messier
- 19c. City or Town: Studio City
- 19d. County: Los Angeles
- 19e. State: California
- Same

PHYSICIAN'S OR CORONER'S CERTIFICATION

- 21a. Coroner: [signature]
- 21b. Date Signed: 12/12/72
- Attending Physician: 12-11-72 / 12-10-72
- Address: 540 N. Central, Glendale
- License No: C-24057

FUNERAL DIRECTOR AND LOCAL REGISTRAR

- 22a. Burial
- 22b. Date: 12/12/72
- 23. Name of Cemetery or Crematory: Mt. Vernon Mem. Pk., Fair Oaks, Calif.
- 24. Embalmer's Signature / License Number: 5184
- 25. Name of Funeral Director: Kiefer & Eyerick Mortuary
- DEC 12 1972

CAUSE OF DEATH

- 29. Part I. Death was caused by:
  - (a) Immediate Cause: Pulmonary Edema — 1 mo
  - (b) Due to or as a consequence of: Hodgkins Disease — 13 mo
  - (c) Due to or as a consequence of:
- 30. Part II. Other Significant Conditions:
- 31. Operation performed: Biopsy — 4 yr

This is to certify that this document is a true copy of the official record filed with the Registrar-Recorder/County Clerk.

Conny B. McCormack
Registrar-Recorder/County Clerk

DEC 1 8 2002
19-669300

DNA seems to clear only Zodiac suspect
New-found evidence may allow genetic profile of '60s killer

Mike Weiss, Chronicle Staff Writer
Tuesday, October 15, 2002

Working with DNA evidence, San Francisco homicide inspectors believe they have cleared the only person police ever named as a suspect in the Zodiac killings that terrorized the Bay Area three decades ago.

Genetic traces from envelopes that contained the serial killer's apocalyptic and police-taunting letters in the 1960s appear to have cleared a school teacher and child molester whom Vallejo police and others once identified as the Zodiac, according to inspectors Kelly Carroll and Michael Maloney.

"Arthur Leigh Allen does not match the partial DNA fingerprint developed from bona fide Zodiac letters," said Carroll.

Allen was named by Vallejo Police Capt. Roy Conway as his department's Zodiac suspect after Allen's death at age 58 in 1992.

Maloney and Carroll, who took over the cold case investigation in 2000, also said they recently discovered additional evidence in the Zodiac case that may soon allow them to create a full DNA profile of the Zodiac, who killed five Bay Area residents in 1968 and 1969.

The killer, who struck in Solano and Napa counties and in San Francisco, sent coded letters announcing his crimes.

The killer's taunting messages to police -- "This is Zodiac speaking" and "I am in control of all things" -- have recently been compared to the tarot card message left for police by the sniper who has killed eight and wounded two more in the

Bruce McGregor Davis, age 26—murderer.

END OF "ZODIAC"

WHO WAS HE?   TWO ZODIACS?

BY GINO VALENTINO

Chapter XI

The Miracle

(1980 – 1984)

In December 1979, I approach my father begging him to help in the upcoming election. He looked at me with a gentle skeptical expression and told me "you know I will always help you in any way possible to be a successful person. After you got arrested, the family name was disgraced. There is no way you can win the election!" My father also said "the candidates and the newspapers will bring up that you pled guilty of vote fraud. Also you have been on probation for three years. By you running in the 1980 election, it will only bring more disgrace to our family name. After my father finished talking to me, I started to cry. I couldn't help myself. I knew my father didn't mean what he said, but he is right I have no chance to win. I am responsible for the shame I brought my family. After this conversation , I just wanted to go away and die!

    I was still living at 421 F Street, that night I had another dream, about winning the election. It was awful. I was sweating. I was dreaming about winning the election and then I woke up realizing it was just a dream. I couldn't go back to bed. I just left the house and started to walk. It was two o'clock in the morning. Walking was always my therapy. Many times I used to walk in the cemetery. The cemetery is my place to think. A quiet place, a peaceful place. This is my medicine !

    The next day I told my mother, being an only child, I was very close to my mother. I was going to run for Councilman in the April election.

I told her my father isn't going to help me and without him I can't win. I'm just lying to myself. I can't win, even if my father helped me. I told my mother that I'm not given up; "God" is helping me. I must try to clear my name and the only way I could do that is to win the election. I am going to win, they can't beat me. It is destiny! Please! Mom tell my father, I need his help!

In January of 1980, many thoughts were going through my mind. It was a very tough decision to make. Day after day, going through my mind, how do I explain to the people about my conviction of vote fraud in 1976? I can't tell them I was innocent. (which I was) I had an idea. I will tell them the truth. I was set up, by my father's enemies. The Chief of Police was hired to get rid of me. Everything he said about me was a lie.

Finally, I file my nomination papers as a candidate in the 1980 election. Now, **I need a miracle**! The newspapers made a fool out of me. They brought up about me getting arrested in 1976 ,also they told the media about my three year probation. The newspapers told the media I did 600 hours of public service. When the people read the newspaper, they certainly are not going to vote for me.

One month, before the election I was very nervous. I campaigned very hard, there was a spiritual force pushing me to keep going. Oh, by the way the Chief of Police gave his resignation. I wonder why! Was he scared I would get elected. There were eight candidates running for two seats. All of them were using my conviction in 1976 to their advantage.

Thank God! The last month, my father changed his mind and started to campaign for me. I was so happy. Maybe, there is still hope for me. I have not finished yet. My father was a very powerful man in Colma.

Many times when I was campaigning, I had to stop myself from crying. It was hard for me because I knew the people were thinking I was a criminal.

COLMA ELECTION NIGHT (1980)

Colma voters turned out in overwhelming numbers.(90% turnout of registered voters) this was the biggest turnout in Colma history! I was so excited. I was trembling. I knew "God" was in my corner, also I remember what Wayne Messier told me, back in 1970, "You will be famous someday!"

The famous celebrity Joe Alioto, ex-Mayor of San Francisco walked in the City Hall with his bodyguards. He wished me good luck. I was happy, but very nervous. The people who ran the election box, finally said "the election is over, lets count the votes." The town hall was full of people. Most of them came to see me lose, so the reign of my father would be destroyed. In 1980, they counted the votes manual. During the counting, I was in last place. A cold chill went through my body. Most of the people were applauding, because I was losing the election. I was so embarrassed. I wanted to hide.

Then the last 20 minutes they called my name continuously. My heart was throbbing. I was so happy. I wanted to yell, but I was in shock!

All the time they were calling my name the room was totally silent, all except for one woman, who kept yelling Oh yeah! Here we go! The mafia is here. Oh yeah! Everyone refrained from making a sound. The person who was calling the names was shocked. My name was called over and over, it didn't stop. Every person in the town hall was speechless. I didn't know if I was first or second. I was so Fucked up, I didn't know where I was. When the voting was over, **I went from last to first. I won**! I couldn't believe it. **I did the impossible!**

People started to congratulate me. Most of them never voted for me. I was so excited. I ran over to my father and hugged him, and was yelling "we did it, we did it. " Mr.Alioto shook my hand and said "I am proud of you and your family." I started to run toward the front door of the town hall, the TV Newscasters.(channels 4 and 7) ran after me. I went outside shouting like the Rocky movie, with both arms extended upward, saying Thank you "God!" I didn't want to speak to channels 4 and 7 , but I did. I told them " You were wrong." A reporter from channel 7 put his microphone next to my mouth. I just pushed it away. No matter what they said about me, tonight I am **The King of Colma.**

That night, I knew all those dreams, actually came true. **This was a first time in California, a candidate ever won a city election**, after he got **arrested** for **vote fraud**, in that city. Therefore, tonight **I made California history**! It's amazing how the human mind works. In 1976 when I got arrested, nobody was talking to me.

Four years later, I won the election, which I had no chance to win. Now, everybody is talking to me. It's amazing how that works! It seems like I disappeared for four years and now I am back. I don't feel like the same person anymore. Most people are hypocrites. I guess that's the way people react. I don't understand that, and probably I never will.

To the reader, did the District Attorney win the case against me? **I don't think so!**

Two months after I got elected, an event took place that was a second highlight of my life in 1980. I was invited to a banquet in San Mateo California. There were a lot of people there, Mayors and Councilmans from different cities in San Mateo County. I went there with my father to the banquet and we were talking to a lot of people. Many people, congratulated me on my amazing election victory. That made me happy and I was proud of myself. I was approached by the Assistant District Attorney he congratulated me, on my winning the election. We started to talk, all of a sudden, he asked me "I have to know, please tell me how did you win the election, after we arrested you four years earlier?" While I was walking closer to him, I was smiling and then I said "**you didn't catch me this time**! He looked at me and he was **speechless**! I slowly walked away. **I was feeling good. I felt so happy.** I got back at that son of a bitch! Naturally, I was lying about what I said to him.

To the reader, this was a happy ending. **Now, do you believe in justice?**

My life has always been a merry-go-round. Every 3 to 4 years, my life goes from good to bad and vice versa.

In 1983, I was appointed Mayor of Colma . **I have beaten the system.** In those days the "Ottoboni name was powerful. Nobody could stop us, not even the famous District Attorney, **Keith Sorenson.**

When my mother died in November 1983, my father didn't know she was dead. I believe subconsciously, he knew she was dead. I tried to keep my father alive, but it was hopeless!I went to my mother's funeral, of all the things I did.(Got arrested, and my involvement with a serial killer.) This was the most horrible thing that ever happened to me. Naturally, I went by myself to the funeral.

My father was losing his mind and I had to put him in a convalescent home. I had no other choice. He wanted to die, he couldn't live without my mother. His leg was amputated and I didn't recognize him anymore, also he didn't recognize me.

Let's get back to my mother's funeral. When my mother died, so did I. If you don't know what I mean, I am sorry. I can't explain it. When my mother died, I was totally lost without her. At the funeral, I was crying hysterically and holding on to the casket handles and I wasn't going to let go. Three people were trying to pull me off the casket. Finally, they got me off the ground, holding me away from getting back to the casket.

I don't even remember who they were. I think one of them was my cousin Glen Dugan. After the funeral I cried every night. I didn't want to live anymore, but I had to take care of my father. Naturally, I thought about all the money I would inherit, so I had to stay alive!

In 1984, my father resigned from the council. He didn't even know it. Later that year I won the town election without campaigning.(That's amazing) The people voted for me in memory of my famous father. Believe it or not, I wanted to lose.

VETERAN COLMA MAYOR RAY OTTOBONI IS DEAD

In August of 1984, my father died. His legend died with him. He was the "**King of Colma** ." He was one of the most powerful men in San Mateo County. At his funeral, there were **powerful Politicians** and **Police Chiefs** from neighboring cities. He was hated by many people, but they admired him. All the Police Departments of San Mateo County, the largest county in northern California, will never forget my father's shooting range. The shooting range was a legend. There will never be another!

In nine months, I lost both of my parents. Being an only child, I felt I was abandoned. My way of forgetting my parent's death is gambling.

I went to San Francisco, California. To purchase a vehicle. In the showcase at the dealership, I saw a yellow car. I found out it was an ExCalibur. It looked like a Duesenberg. It was a long car with horns on both sides. I liked it right away. I paid $55,000 in cash. When I drove the car home, I felt like a pimp!

When I got home, I parked the car in the driveway. I lived at 417 F street, the house I grew up in. My neighbor asked me "what the hell is that?" I told him it was a Chevrolet. He was staring at the car saying, "It's not a Chevrolet." I didn't lie to him; the car's engine was made by Chevrolet.

The next crazy thing I did in 1984, was get married. I knew Denise about five years. Both of us were from different worlds. I was all Fucked up, and I needed someone. Hopefully, Denise would help me get by my tragedy. I had to sign a prenuptial note. I bought Denise a used Mercedes-Benz. We got married in Nevada. She was sick that day and I was mentally sick for marrying her. Anyway, the marriage was terrible and I finally realized this woman was not going to help me with my problems. We lived at 417 F street in Colma. We had many arguments. One night she called the police on me. I didn't do anything to her. What was the police going to do to me? I still had a lot of power even without my father. The marriage lasted three months. She got the Mercedes-Benz and a lot of money. I don't remember how much. I paid her alimony for one year, I wasn't mad at her. I'm just glad to be rid of her!

Chapter XII

"Cowboy"

In January 1985, both my parents were dead. I inherited a lot of money. I couldn't live in Colma anymore, because of all the terrible memories. So I moved to Sparks, Nevada. The first trip I rented a truck. I brought with me all my father's guns, rifles and shotguns. Between all of them there were over 100 guns.

The second trip I drove the ExCalibur to Sparks. The next day I went to a western store named Parker's. It was famous for having the best Western apparel in Reno, Nevada. I bought cowboy pants, shirts and a gold buckle. I purchased two cowboy hats. I felt like a million bucks.

I had many snake hat bands. When I wore them on my Western hats, I had that exotic look. Many times I scared women away from me. They thought I was a pimp, or a drug dealer.

When I came to Nevada, I was a different person. I liked women and I treated them good. I used them for sex, and then I got rid of them. I thought Nevada women were all sluts! I had no respect for anybody. I guess I was getting back at society. Loss of my mother made me angry, I took my anger out on people. That was wrong! I've always been a loner. Since I lost my parents, I became a monster.

Many times I thought of Wayne Messier, the "Zodiac" killer, also I was thinking of becoming the "Zodiac" serial killer. Quickly, I erased that thought from my mind. I knew that I needed to get rid of those terrible thoughts. The answer was gambling! When I am watching a sport event and I have money on it, I don't remember or think about anything. That was my medicine. It cost me millions of dollars, but it kept me alive! **You the reader**, tell me what was the answer? I honestly believe whatever I would have done, it would have ended in a disaster. Come on, am I right or wrong? I have to know the answer!

Five months ago, I purchased 4 racing horses, two of them were from Argentina. My trainer was Dale Steward. I Had bad luck with all of my horses. Two of them died and the other two broke down. I remember going to Hollywood racetrack and watching a particular horse run. Down the stretch, Raise a Legend won the race. That horse was in a claiming race. No one claimed him!

One month later, I saw the same horse racing in another claiming race. This time I had my trainer, Dale Steward, come with me to Hollywood racetrack and I gave him $25,000 to claim that horse. That means when the race starts, unless someone else claims that horse, no matter what happens to that horse. I'm the owner of that horse! The horse won the race. The name of the horse was Raise a Legend. I was happy. It was just for a short time!

Two weeks later, I ran the horse in Bay Meadows racetrack, in California. Russell Base was the jockey. Turning for home, my horse pulled up lame, and never ran again. One of the other horses, from Argentina, died having a baby.

You the reader, do you think I was cursed? Be careful, I can read your mind.

Also in 1985, I took acting lessons in Studio City, California. I hated Los Angeles. I drove my ExCalibur to Los Angeles. I met a man in a gas station. I pulled up in my ExCalibur, and parked next to his car. As he was putting gasoline in his car he came over to talk to me. He said "I like your car; I never saw a car like that. Is it an American car?" I told him "yes it is. The name of the car is an ExCalibur. I called it my Pimp Mobile!" He started to laugh, and replied "my name is Joe Drago. I said "you are an Italian, So am I. My name is Ray." He admired my car, and he was very friendly. Joe gave me his card and told me he was the owner of the Fisherman, a famous bar in Beverly Hills. I knew Beverly Hills was a famous city in Los Angeles, that's where all the movie stars live.

I was heading back to my apartment building, which was called Marina Del Rey apartments, a rich and expensive area. I got off on Santa Monica Blvd. I realized I made a mistake, because I was lost. I was trying to turn around and go back the way I came. I found myself in a bad area, there were young black kids walking on the sidewalk, dressed up just like gang members. I was driving my Pimp Mobile in this bad area. Oh God! Please get me out of here. Do I go back, or do I go straight ahead? I had a gun in the car, but I am a sitting target. I am totally fucked. Finally, I saw a police vehicle going the opposite direction. I immediately made a U-turn, now I am behind the police vehicle. I am following the police vehicle everywhere he went. Finally, the police vehicle slowed down. The only thing I thought of is to beap my horn. The officer moved over and let me pass him, and then he put his red lights on.

I was so happy I could cry I moved off the roadway, and rolled down my window. The officer approached my car and said "What is wrong." I told him I am lost and I want to go to Marina Del Rey. The officer asked me "what am I doing in this area with this car!" I told him I took the wrong exit off the freeway. The officer said "Follow me." The officer never asked me for my driver's license. That's unbelievable! I got back on the freeway and went straight to the apartment. I was lucky I didn't get killed.

That night, I had to go and see where the Fisherman is located. I was dressed to kill. I looked like a rich man and I was. I called up the Fisherman, and got directions. I don't want to get lost at night, especially with the Pimp Mobile. I got to the Fisherman, it was a fancy bar. The cars that were parked on the street were Rolls Royce, Jaguar and Mercedes Benz. Those cars were very expensive.

The Pimp Mobile can't compete with these cars. I parked the car behind the Rolls-Royce. I felt out of place walking in looking like a cowboy. Oh, fuck It! I went in and started looking for Joe. I saw Joe waving for me to come over. He introduced me to Barbara Eden. (I Dream of Jennie) she was very sexy. I felt like a jackass, wearing a cowboy hat and coat. Joe introduced me to Lee Marvin; he was sitting in a booth with friends. I stayed about an hour. Just in time to

see four people carrying Lee Marvin out the front door. He was totally intoxicated. I always liked Lee Marvin, no matter how drunk he was. That night, when I was driving home, I was thinking what goes through the mind of a popular movie star to make a complete ass out of himself.

The next day, I drove back to Reno. I still had $300,000 in the safe deposit box in Colma, California. So far I have control of my gambling, but that would quickly change. I was going to inherit a lot of money. (Millions of Dollars) before I came to Reno, I was a big gambler. Now, I'm in a 24 hours city where gambling is legal. I'm in heaven, or was it hell!

In early of 1986, I drove to Colma to get the 300,000 that was in the bank. I immediatly went to San Francisco, to buy another car. I purchased a 1984 Rolls Royce. It cost me $80,000. I always wanted to drive a Rolls Royce. The car was a major problem. The Rolls was always in the body shop, it had major electronic problems. The Excalibur was a fun car, but the Rolls was my luxury car. It also had a car phone, but it had something the ExCalibur didn't have. Can you guess what that was? **Come on reader**, think, I will give you a hint! I had it installed in the back seat of the Rolls. **Yes**! **You got it**, that didn't take long. A television set with a VCR. I never had a problem with the TV set. My friend, Jack did all the driving, can you imagine the fun I had in the back seat with the ladies. Also, can you imagine what movies I was playing? I am sweating thinking about it. I purchased a fancy house in southwest Reno. I had all the tools. I had two fancy cars. I dress like a cowboy. I had women chasing me everywhere, but it still wasn't enough.

My nickname "**Cowboy** started when different people started calling me "Cowboy" Reno is a small city, so the name "Cowboy" got around to every casino. No one ever knew my name. The pit bosses, of the casino called me Mr. "O."

Reno, Sparks and LakeTahoe always knew who I was, especially when I walked into the casino!

My friend Jack Lantz, he taught me how to play craps. Again that was my demise! He was with me all the time.

I had the cars, money and fame. Was that enough! No, it wasn't. I was an **extremist**. When I did something, I went all the way. I wore six rings, three on one hand and three on the other hand. One of the rings was my father's ring. It had the number "50" on it. I put diamonds, emeralds and rubies on the number "50." It looked fantastic. One particular ring, on my left hand, was my personal ring. It had the letters "DL." In memory of Donna Lass. She was killed in 1970, by the "Zodiac" killer. I wasn't finished just yet! I had to have more jewelry. I wore a gold chain with a large pendant. I placed a picture of my car, the ExCalibur on the pendant. I put diamonds and rubies on the car. It was stunning, it was unique! I looked like a pimp or drug dealer. Or both! Believe me, I wasn't showing off. I was just trying to impress myself.

I was at Bally's casino watching a baseball game. I made a $7000 bet on the Chicago Cubs. The New York Mets scored two runs in the last of the ninth inning to win the game. I lost another fucking bet. I went crazy I took an empty beer bottle and threw it at the large television screen. When the beer bottle hit the screen, it made a hole in the bottom of the television screen. The security guards came and escorted me out. One of the guards said, "Please, come back tomorrow "Cowboy," if you don't I'll be fired." It's amazing, I could do anything I wanted and nothing would happen to me. The "Cowboy" was famous for betting and losing a lot of money.

I made an $8000 bet on a baseball game. I bet on the Detroit Tigers against Chicago White Sox. Usually, I watched the game at my house, but this time I was at Bally's casino. I was talking to a cocktail waitress, I decided to watch the game at the casino. I was winning. Detroit was leading 3 to 0. Chicago scored five runs in the fifth inning. Chicago was ahead 5 to 3 going into the sixth inning. I was so fucken mad. When I make a sport bet I took it personally. That is because I am a sick gambler.

There was one person betting for Chicago. He was yelling and making loud noises. It was driving me crazy. I went up to him, asking him . I told him to leave the sports casino. He told me "I don't have to leave. I haven't done anything wrong, I have seen you before." You are the "Cowboy." I told him, you bet $10 on this fucken game. I'll give you $200 to get the fuck out of here. He replied give me the $200 and I will leave. I gave him the $200; he immediately left the sports casino. I lost the fucking game 5 to 4. I lost $8000, plus the $200 that I gave him. Also he won his $10 bet. I left the casino mad, because I gave the kid $200 to leave the casino. I didn't care about losing the $8000. Am I crazy or just plain stupid?

Later in 1986, started my downfall in gambling. I had a lot of money and my sport betting increased. The MGM is gone and now it is called Bally's. I had markers in five different casinos. When the casino give someone a credit line, that is called a marker. The biggest credit line I had was in Bally's casino. It was $50,000. It escalated to 100,000.

I wasn't just a normal person. I wore an abundance of jewelry on my fingers. I drove two expensive cars. One of the cars was exotic. I spent an extreme amount of money in sport betting. Also I bet a lot of money in craps. What I am trying to say is that I was exposed to great danger. At night, especially in that exotic car, I was vulnerable to getting robbed or killed. All the time, I had two guns in my ExCalibur Thank God, I never got robbed, but I came close!

- This happened on a Friday night, around two o'clock in the morning. Before I left Bally's casino, I took my gun case from the trunk and put it on the passenger seat. I was driving my ExCalibur to my house in southwest Reno. I noticed a car, in my rear view mirror, following me. Every turn I made, the car behind me followed. I was getting worried. I was driving west on Plum street, passing Virginia street. If you are not familiar with my car, the interior is very small and there isn't too much room. The car has bucket seats, and the back seat is close to the front seat. The trunk is tiny. So all the weight and length, is on the front of the car. It is very difficult to see on both sides of the car! I made a left turn onto Hunter Lake.

-
- The car is still following me. Then I made a right turn and then a left turn onto Susileed drive, that's where I lived. At this time I'm getting scared. It's not a policeman, so why is this car following me. I know I am helpless in my car, it is like a death trap. I passed my house and I went straight up the hill. I was still on Susileed. I made a right turn and circled around coming back onto Susileed. Only this time I am going down the Hill. That fucking car is still behind me keeping his distance. As they came closer to my house, which is to the right of me, I made a quick right turn into my driveway. I had to get out of the car, because if I didn't I'm a dead man. I didn't want to go in my garage, because I wouldn't be able to see that car. That fucking car stopped next to my driveway. I opened the gun case, took out the **UZI**,(Israeli military pistol, 9 mm hand-held lightweight semi-automatic submachine gun) then I put the magazine in the machine gun.

I got out of the car and went behind the car door I put a cartridge in the chamber. When I looked up the car was still there! My rear lights were on so I could see everything that went on. Suddenly, I observed both men getting out of the car. I could see both men **were armed**. They were hiding behind their car doors; all of a sudden they **started shooting**. I hesitated to shoot, because the UZI would kill everyone in the car. I could hear their **bullets** hit something. Then as quickly as it started it was over.

- They got back in their car and left. I felt relieved they were gone and I was still alive. I unloaded the UZI and put it back in the case I walked around the car and saw it had been hit, also the garage door had been hit. Quickly I put the UZI, that was in the case, on the passenger seat.

- I got in the car and quickly drove into the garage. I got my

45 automatic pistol out of the glove compartment, cocked it and got out of the car. I locked the garage door, then went out to rear of the garage and went in the back door of the house ,taking my trained attack dog Kato in the house with me. I never called the police because I could not identify the man or the car. What a fucking night. Someday the pimp mobile is going to get me **killed**.

I used to patronize all the brothels in the outskirts of Reno and Carson City, Nevada. Sometimes every other day. Jack and I was their best customer. I had other friends I took to get laid. It's amazing, I've been going to the whore house for two years and no matter who I took I paid for. I didn't like the whore houses. But all the money I was losing, I needed to escape from gambling.

The only thing I wanted from those women was a massage. If I wanted a woman, I didn't have go to the brothel to get laid. I have more women after me that I could handle. I was turning most of the women away. I was physically and emotionally exhausted from losing, between ten or twenty thousand dollars a day.

To the reader, I hate to talk about my erratic behavior, but this story is about my life as a gambler. So I have to tell the truth. When I am watching a sporting event and I have a large sum of money on the game, I am a complete basket case. I'm very superstitious! One night, a blackjack dealer was over at my house for dinner. We were having sex in the bedroom, I looked at the clock and it was almost 8 o'clock. My football game was coming on at 8 o'clock. I stopped having sex and jumped out of bed and told her I was sorry but I have to watch my football game. She got mad, and didn't know what to say!

I immediately went to the living room and turned on the game. She was furious and started calling me dirty names. I told her we can continue at a later date. After I said that I went to the living room and turned on the television set. I was watching the football game then I started to take all my clothes off. She came out from the bedroom fully clothed. She said very angrily, "what the fuck are you doing." I was completely nude holding a loaded revolver and was pacing back and forth. She went screaming toward the front door saying, "you are a fucking lunatic." After she left I went inside the furnace nude, to watch the game, hoping to give me luck. Anyway, I lost the game and then I shot the television set. That was a normal day for me. I wonder what **the reader** thinks of me now. This is nothing, **just wait it gets real bad**!

It was 10 o'clock on a Saturday night, I was alone, just me and my dog Kato. When I heard a knock on my door I put Kato in the backyard. Kato was a attack trained dog. He ready bit two people, so I had to be careful. I look to see who it was. It was a woman, I knew her from the brothel. I opened the door and she said "Cowboy, I need your help, please help me!" I asked her if she needs money. She replied, "No, my girlfriend is in the car and she is hurt." I closed the front door and we walked to her car. I opened the passenger door of the Volkswagen, I saw a girl covered with blood on her face. I told the other girl to take her to the hospital. She was crying and said, "I can't, she was beaten by her boyfriend." I stared at her saying, "is her boyfriend a pimp!" The girl looked at me and was speechless.

I hated pimps, they are nothing but bloodsucking parasites. I got the girl out of the car and carried her in my house. There was blood on me. Someone hit her on the nose and there was a bruise on her eye. I put her on my sofa. I went to the bathroom to get peroxide and cotton. I was thinking about all the prostitutes, coming to me for money, trying to get away from their pimps. I learned a lot about the prostitutes and their pimps. The girls want to be dominated by the pimp. They want to give their money to the pimp. The pimp controls them by fear! The girls are so insecure, they are proud to have a pimp. Anyway, when the girls leave, most of them go back to the pimp.

To the reader, remember I told you this story becomes more **unbelievable and terrifying! So don't stop now. Keep reading.**

Let me tell you something that will blow your mind. Jack and I was at Kitty's, the brothel in Carson City, Nevada. That night, there weren't many customers. So the girls came out talked to the customer. It's amazing, Jack was sixty-six years old, and was fucking every time. The cowboy was different, I didn't like prostitutes. I went there to get a massage and to get away from the casino. Jack was twenty years older than me and he loved to have sex. Don't get the wrong idea. The "Cowboy" could fuck for hours. I don't know why I lasted that long. I was a gambler that was my sex. **I'm sorry; I forgot what I was going to tell you**, see what happens when I talk about gambling. I remembered what it was! **Are you ready**? That night, I noticed a girl was in the room for a long time with a customer. When she came out and sat on the couch, I went over and sat next to her. I asked her if she's having a good night. She told me she just made $5000. I look at her and said "what did you do to make that much money." She wouldn't tell me. I knew the manager of the brothel, every time she went to Bally's casino, I would get her a free hotel room. I got up from the couch and walked over to the cashier's cage. I saw the manager and asked her, what did that girl do to make $5000? The manager doesn't tell anybody what happened between the girl and the customer. Those are the rules. Only the "Cowboy" could get that information. The "Cowboy" was like a **"God"** in his heyday. The manager told me that the girl had to dress up in a chicken costume. The customer was running around the room trying to catch the girl, in the chicken costume. When he catches the girl, in his mind he is **fucking the chicken**, not the girl. After talking to the manager. I walked away thinking, **nothing wrong with him**!

Let's talk about someone else. I used to go to the casinos with David Jenkins, a good friend. He loved to gamble. David and I go back and longtime, I knew him when I was Chief of Police in Colma, California. He was amazing in playing craps. When he was hot, he was unstoppable. I remember two times, he was fantastic. When the Virginia Casino first opened up, I made a lot of money. David held the dice for a long time. The second time, we were at Eddie's, the Fabulous Fifties casino, David was the shooter, he held the dice a long time. I made over $50,000 that day. Unfortunately, I was getting destroyed in my sport betting.

In 1987, my ex-wife, Linda called me and asked if I could send her some money. She needed more money to support the children. I never asked her any questions I just sent her what she wanted. The same day I went to Western Union and telegraphed her the money. Many times I telegraphed money through Western Union to my daughter. I always took care of my children, I send them money. I never grew up with them, so I just gave them money. It's terrible for a parent to get old. Knowing he doesn't have a family.

I almost forgot to talk about another good friend. Her name was Denise Gonderman, she was an interesting woman. She was a tomboy. Any man that said anything bad about her or me, she would knock him out! Denise was honest and reliable. I always had fun with Denise, she was a true friend. After her ex-husband died, she went back to Santa Maria, California. I missed Denise!

David Vallerga, my best friend, we go back a long time. He was very strong and tough; no one beat David in a fight. Since 1985, David visited Reno many times. We had fun gambling and talking about the good old days. He was very knowledgeable with pistols. In my opinion David could take a pistol apart and put it back together. He taught me everything

I knew about guns. He was the master. David still lives in northern California, with his wife. He doesn't come to Reno anymore. I still love him like a brother.

I collected Thousand Dollar bills; it was a hobby of mine. I had seven Thousand Dollar bills on me at all times. It wasn't a power trip, I always liked things that are unique. Not many people knew I carried Thousands Dollar bills.

I had a lot of money; I could get anything I wanted. It's terrible to say that, but it's the truth. In 1987, I had a doctor which I could get any drug I needed. I got tranquilizers from him. I didn't take any other drugs. I had a pharmacist, which he gave me tranquilizers. I didn't need a prescription. Also he gave me antibiotics. I gave generous tips to both the doctor and the pharmacist. Money buys anybody and everything.

Later in 1987, I got a mystery phone call. The person calling was angry and was yelling at me. He said "Are you the cowboy?" I asked him, "Who are you?" He answered, "**None of your fucking business.**" I was going to hang up and then in an angry voice he said, "**Stay away from my girls**." Right away I knew this mother fucker is a pimp. I hate pimps! I replied, "No one tells me what to do, especially a fucking pimp." He started threatening me. I had enough, couldn't take anymore. I told him I will meet him tonight and we will finish this conversation. We were going to meet at 10 o'clock that night, down the hill from where I live. It's a dark secluded place. The pimp hung up on me. I believe he thought I was a pimp and I was going to take his girls away from him. Between the jewelry I wore and the pimp car. I can understand why he thought I was a pimp! Immediately, I called up Jack and told him I needed him tonight, come over about 9 o'clock. Jack said, "What's going on Cowboy?" I told Jack, I didn't want to talk about it. I said, "Be at my house at 9 o'clock."

When Jack arrived at my house, I told him what happened. I could tell he was scared. I told him I needed his help. He smiled and said, "What do you want me to do." I didn't know what to tell him. So, calmly I replied, "Tonight, you are going to drive the Rolls, I will be in the backseat with the UZI (submachine gun)" Jack asked me "What the fuck are you going to do with the UZI?" I was laughing, when I told him "I'm going to kill a pimp!" Jack thought I was kidding, but I wasn't. We left at ten minutes to 10. I put the **magazine in the machine gun**. I was thinking of the old days, when the mob had someone in the backseat with a Thompson submachine gun. When we got to the destination, where the pimp was going to meet us. I told Jack just drive around the area. He drove around twice and then I told him park the Rolls on the opposite side of the street.

We saw a car coming; it turned around and parked on the opposite side of the street. It had to be the pimp! I knew Jack was frightened. I didn't want him to get involved in a murder. I told Jack not to take any marijuana with him. He never listens to me. Jack, I am getting sick smelling that marijuana, you know I have asthma. You are going to get us killed. Jack asked me, "What do we do now?" I replied, "I don't know!" All of the sudden, someone in the backseat, of that car, started to open the window.

I immediately, said to Jack don't be scared, start the car and lay down on your right side. Jack was fucken scared. **I put a cartridge in the chamber.** I wanted to show that pimp, that I meant business. I felt real powerful, like the " **Zodiac Killer.**" I couldn't wait any longer. I had to do something now! I told Jack to get up and drive slowly by the car. Jack was frightened, I tried to calm Jack down by saying, don't be scared, I'm not going to do anything. As Jack was driving past the car, I opened the back window, pointed the UZI at the car. I had one knee on the seat; I aimed at the back tire. I fired three or four rounds, hitting the car door and the rear tire. The car left at a high rate of speed. I was yelling at Jack, "Let's get the hell out of here." Whoever was in that car had to be scared to death! We went back to my house . It was an **exciting night**.

A week later, I went back to the brothel in Carson City, Nevada, just to see if any of his girls were working. I saw one of them; I approached her and said, "Tell your pimp, if he calls me again he's a dead man. Do I make myself clear?" Later, I found out the **pimp left Nevada**. In those days, no one **FUCKED** with the **COWBOY**!

Everyone called me the "Cowboy" because I looked and dressed like one! In California, I used to go dancing in western nightclubs. Unfortunately, the people that knew me didn't know the good things I did for people. I helped many **prostitutes** to leave their **pimps**! I don't know why I helped them. I guess I felt sorry for them. I was there savior. The pimps knew of me, and what I was capable of doing to them. I remember I beat up a pimp so bad, that he left Nevada. I hit him with steel lined gloves. I knew he couldn't go to the police. **I hated pimps**, luckily I didn't kill one, but I came close! I was a **bounty hunter,** chasing after pimps. I took no money from the prostitutes. When I left Reno in 1989, the pimps were happy to see me leave.

If I didn't write the story, nobody would have known the good things

I did for those women! I knew many of the prostitutes from all the brothel most of them were from the brothel in Carson City. They got in trouble with the police on their days off. They called me up and I bailed them out of jail. I don't remember how many girls I bailed out. I used to drive the ExCalibur to the jail on Par Boulevard. I remember, one girl needed $5000, to get home. I gave her the money. If I think about the things I did for the prostitutes, I guess I was their pimp. As I said before I never took any money from them. That's why I called the ExCalibur, the Pimp Mobile.

Later that week, approx. 2 am in the morning, I got a visitor. It was the Judge and he was drinking! Bill was the Judge of the municipal court. I knew he couldn't go home, he didn't want his wife to see him drunk. The judge has been to my house before. He slept in the upstairs room. Bill did favors for me, so I didn't mind helping him!

The "Cowboy" knew everybody. He was powerful! He knew judges, policemen and the Mayor of Reno.

In 1985, a documentary movie was filmed about me, it was called the "King of Colma". Later I became The "King of Reno". Isn't that amazing!

One Night, I took the judge to the brothel in Carson City. I drove my Excalibur. The Judge was scared that somebody would recognize him. I gave him my cowboy hat. He looked like a real cowboy! I told him no one will recognize you! Finally, he felt comfortable. When we arrived at the brothels, I could see he wasn't happy. I was always a master of disguise. I got out of my car and opened the trunk. I pick up something from my suitcase and then I got back in the car. When the judge saw what I bought him, he was in shock! I placed the patch over his left eye. I started to laugh, then I said nobody will recognize you! When we walked in, two girls came over to me. Naturally, the girls all knew who I was.

When we sat down on the couch, the judge started talking to this girl, she was a knock-out! Quickly, they got up and went to her room. I got up and whisper in his ear, "watch your money"! When the judge came back from the room, he looked happy, so I knew he got what he wanted! We left the brothel and I was driving back to Reno I got pulled over by a police officer. The judge already took off the patch on his eye, but was still wearing my cowboy hat. I got out of the Excalibur, so the officer couldn't see the judge.

It was a Reno police officer and he told me I was speeding! I knew

I was getting a speeding ticket, especially, driving the pimp mobile. The officer gave me a ticket and told me to drive carefully. When I got back in the car, I told the judge that fucking cop gave me a ticket because I was driving that car! The judge agreed with me. He took the ticket and told me he would take of it! Also he told me he enjoyed himself and would like to do this again. That made my day!

In the summer 1988, Jack and I played craps many times at the flamingo casino.

One day, I was introduced to Tom Wirshing, he was the manager of the casino. We talked about my gambling problem. He couldn't believe I was losing money in astronomical numbers! He was a professional in his job, also a pleasant man to talk to.

One day, Jack and I was gambling at the Flamingo casino and I saw Tom and I decided to take him gambling after he gets off work. He didn't want to go! I asked him why? He told me, when he played craps he never threw the dices. Also he stated he was a terrible shooter. After he told me that story, I didn't know what to say!

Finally, I convince, him to come with us! We all met at 8 o'clock at the Flamingo and than we went to the Virginia Casino. I gave Tom fifty dollars, and he was the first person to roll the dices. I could tell he didn't want to throw the dices. Anyway, he threw the dices for 45 minutes. It was unbelievable! I was betting the limit. I was so happy, I was kissing him! I was jumping up and down like a maniac. Tom was so excited, he was getting a adrenalin rush! The casino was crowded and the security guards were behind us, protecting us from the undesirables!

Tom pick up the dices, took a deep breath, and he threw the dices for 40 minutes. That's incredible I was getting tired of yelling and screaming and I knew it was time to quit! I won fifty thousand dollars, I gave Jack one thousand dollars, tom won six hundred dollars. I offered Tom two thousand dollars, he didn't want the money. He told me it was bad luck! (Today, Tom is the manager of casino marketing at the Silver Legacy Casino in Reno, Nevada.) I asked Tom if he would like to go to the brothel. He told me he was married, also he doesn't cheat on his wife! We all left the Casino happy. My good luck will be gone and forgotten! <u>Keep</u> <u>Reading</u>!

Many times on a Friday night, Jack and I went to Caesar's casino in Lake Tahoe, Nevada. We ate and gambled. Then on the way back we stopped at the brothels in the outskirts of Carson City, Nevada. I never will forget the one remarkable day. It was like it never happened. We left on a Friday night around 5 o'clock, heading for Lake Tahoe. I was driving my ExCalibur. I was driving through Carson City and in my rear view mirror I saw a police vehicle flashing his red lights on me.(That night I took the top off the Excalibur) I was scared, Jack was stoned on marijuana. Thank God, the top was down so the police officer could not smell it. As the police officer approached me, he said I was going too fast. He told me to get out of the car. I was happy because Jack was stoned. I got out of the car and I was walking to the back of my car, following the police officer. He asked me for my driver's license. I know I was getting a speeding ticket, police hated my car. The officer told me his wife is a blackjack dealer at the Peppermill Casino, and she always tells me about the famous "Cowboy." He asked me "Where is your hat." I told him it's in the backseat. I was amazed at what he was telling me. The officer said, "Could you do me a favor?" I didn't know what to say. Naturally, I was stuttering.

The officer said "Can I have your autograph, it's for my wife." I was in shock. I thought he was joking, but he wasn't. I signed my name writing it on his scratch pad. **That's unbelievable**! I got back in my car and told Jack what happened. Jack was amazed, but he was so stoned, I don't think he knew where he was. When we arrived at Caesar's casino, I was hungry so we went to the Chinese restaurant. I loved Chinese food. After we ate, we went straight to the crap table. We played about an hour and I lost $10,000 . I told Jack let's get the fuck out of here!

We left Lake Tahoe and drove to the Kit Kat, the brothel in Carson City. I know most of the girls. Jack was friendly with all of the girls. He liked black women. A gorgeous black lady came up to me and started talking. I was not in a good frame of mind. She asked me, "Are you having a good time." I replied, "I lost a lot of money tonight." While we were talking, Jack came over and started talking to her. Jack told me to take her to the room. I stared at Jack and said, "I don't fuck a white prostitute, why would I fuck a black prostitute? Jack looked at me saying, it might change your luck. Jack already knows I don't believe in that bullshit. I had an idea. I turned to the black girl saying, "Do you want to go to a casino and gamble?" She asked me how many hours?(This is called an out date) I told her 4 or 5 hours. she replied, "That would be $600." I smiled and replied ,okay I'll send you back in a cab. Usually, you have to show your driver's license, but the manager of the brothel knows me.

When we got outside she saw the Excalibur, and she asked what kind car is that? She was excited to get into the car. Jack got in the back with the girl. When we got to Bally's casino. I told Jack, the black girl is with you. I looked at the girl and said, "I'm sorry that's the way it has to be." I tried to make her comfortable. I don't date black women, that's my choice! She didn't care, it's all about money! **To the reader**, I'm sorry, I forgot to tell you that I gave the girl $600 ,before we left the brothel.

It is about 11 o'clock at night, there's one person on the crap table. Jack was next to the girl I was on the other end of the table. I asked for a marker for $20,000, my limit was $100,000. When I got the chips, I gave the girl and Jack $1000 each to play crap. What happened next is better than having a sexual orgasm. **To the reader**, You don't believe that do you! That girl rolled the dices for approximately an hour, without crapping out. I won over $50,000. I tipped the dealers $1000. I gave the girl $5000 and I gave Jack $2000. Jack said, "See Cowboy, I was right she changed your luck. Jack asked me if I could get a room for him and the girl. I gave Jack $1000 more to pay for the girl for staying overnight. I went home a winner. I couldn't sleep, thinking did the black girl really change my luck? **To the reader**,what do you think, did she change my luck?

In the winter 1987, on a Friday afternoon. How did I remember that! Well, because I want a lot of money on the crap game. That day, everything I did on the crap game went my way. Jack and I was on the crap game at the Peppermill Casino. Jack was throwing the dice and I was betting $1000 on every roll. The dice is like a woman, it can turn on you in a split second. The crap table was full of people, most of the time that is good. You never know when a hot shooter is going to roll. Jack wasn't hot or cold. The dice wasn't helping me win. The dice is unpredictable! Okay, it's my turn to throw the dice. Usually, I am very unlucky when I throw the dice.

I started to make bigger bets. I was making my number, over and over. I was placing my bets. If you don't understand what I'm talking about? It's okay. Who cares! Back to the crap game, I was fucking hot, everything I did was right. When you're on a roll, you start talking to the dice. "Come on dice. Be nice!" I had $5000 on the crap table. Over and over I made my number. The pit boss was getting nervous. Another pit boss came and he was getting worried. I held the dice for close to an hour. Both pit bosses were watching me and so was the eye in the sky(security upstairs). I won $70,000 that day, the most money I ever won on the crap game. That day I was **King of the Dice**! Remember, I was losing about $20,000 a day in sport betting!

To the reader, the next **four years** were disasters. I dealt with tragedy events with unhappy endings. I didn't want to talk about the events that happened in those years. But this story is about the rise and fall of a legend!

So I have to tell **the reader** everything that happened. I cried many times writing this story.

In 1988, I was losing approximately $50,000 a week in betting sports. It is amazing, I just keep gambling and losing. I never took a break. At night, I went with Jack to the brothel, to escape from gambling. Most of the time we went to the brothel in Carson City, Nevada.

The Cowboy was famous for spending a lot of money and living the life of a King. Also I was known for giving money to people. For example, a girl that was a blackjack dealer. I only met her once! I gave her $5000 to buy furniture for her house. I hated women, but I help them. I can understand why! I will never know the answer!

The last three months of 1988 were pathetic! I made three large sport bets. One bet was **astronomical**. I lost all **three bets**. That's incredible. It was impossible to lose all three bets. The curse of my grandmother was to powerful. I know you don't know what I'm talking about. My grandmother put a spell on my gambling, she had mystical powers. I hate my grandmother for putting that curse on me. **To the reader**, Do you think I'm crazy. I'm not making this up about my grandmother. I went through millions of dollars. Sometimes, I went twenty days without winning a sport bet. Today, I still have my grandmother's curse! You still believe I'm crazy? I am sorry I forgot to tell you who the teams were, that I bet on! And how much I bet on them. I took the Oakland Athletics against los Angeles Dodgers in the World Series in 1988. Oakland was favored 3 to 1. I had five people betting for me. I had $360,000 on the World Series. Also I bet more money on Oakland, the second game of the World Series. That was when Kirt Gibson was injured, he hit the home run in the ninth inning to win the game! I had $80,000 on that game I immediately took my 45 automatic pistol and fired three or four rounds into the television set.(That was my second bet)

The next day I bought another large television set. Los Angeles won the World Series, so I lost $440,000.

Two months later, my third bet was on the Super Bowl! I bet $120,000, and took the Denver Broncos against the Washington Redskins! I lost that bet to! Doug Williams, quarterback of Washington, played his best game of his career! In three months, just in sports betting only I lost $560,000! That's why the **"Cowboy"** became famous. No one could compete with him.

Between 1986 and 1988, I shot three television sets in my house! I was a violent loser. I never hurt no one, but I took my hostile behavior off on the television. One time I broke my heel by kicking the television set. I had millions of dollars, but when I lost the games,(football, baseball) I took it personal. It wasn't about money. I had plenty of that. Gambling is all about the excitement of winning or losing! Gambling is similar to alcohol and drugs. I was an **adrenalin junkie**

I had enough punishment. I had to leave Reno, before I go broke! I was going to Tucson Arizona where my son and daughter live with their mother. The Cowboy couldn't just leave Reno without having a going away party. I picked the Peppermill Casino, because it was famous for its food. David Jenkins worked at the Peppermill as a chief, so it only cost me $10,000, instead of $20,000. The food was excellent and the party room was full of people. It was the largest party that the city of Reno ever had. Everybody came to the party, even people I didn't know, but I don't care! My family was there from Arizona, that made me feel good. Many people at the party told me the "Cowboy" will never be forgotten.

In 1989, I headed for Tucson, Arizona. I drove my old truck to Arizona. My Excalibur and Rolls Royce were transported to Tucson. I was very sad to leave Reno, but I had to leave, I had lost millions of dollars in the casino. I had no other choice!

I bought a new house in Tucson and a week later my two cars arrived from Reno. I was happy to see my son and daughter. Naturally, they asked me for money. I gave them money, that's what a rich father does. I gave my daughter more money, because I was much closer to her. It's very hot in Tucson in the summer and there is nothing to do there. I don't know what to do with myself, and that became a major problem. I've been in Tucson four month and I had an automobile accident with the ExCalibur. It was my fault; I made a right turn not looking at the car ahead of me. It is very difficult to see in the car from either side. Anyway, it was my fault. Hardly any damage to the other car. My car, the front was demolished. It had to be towed. I hit my head on the windshield. Contacted my ex-wife, and she took me to the hospital. I had a headache, they gave me pain pills I was worried about my car.

The body shop told me they had to order the parts, from where the car was built. The car was built in Wisconsin. It took three months to fix the damage. I was so fucking mad at myself. The color of the car was yellow and I had it changed to brown and orange, **do you believe that!** When they finish painting the car, it looked different. The car didn't look like the Pimp Mobile. The color looked awful. I fucked up!

In the autumn of 1989, I was watching the World Series on television, during the game there was a major earthquake in San Francisco, California. I got up from the sofa and I remember saying "Oh my God, Oh no!" I didn't know what to do. I just hope the earthquake didn't hit Colma. I couldn't sleep that night, so the next day I contacted my insurance agent, which was located in the Daly City, California, north of Colma. He told me four houses were damaged by the earthquake. Also people were injured.

After the insurance agent finished talking, I knew that I was totally fucked. I didn't have any earthquake insurance. After taking a deep breath, I knew I'm going to need a lawyer. I was sick to my stomach and by not having earthquake insurance, this tragedy is going to cost me millions of dollars!

After this nightmare was over, between the lawsuits and the attorneys, it cost me approximately $3 million dollar!

I didn't stay in Arizona long. In 1990 I sold the house and moved to Washington. I wanted to go to Canada but I decided it was too cold. I drove the Rolls-Royce and the ExCalibur was transported to Washington. It was winter in Washington, and it rained every day! All the time I lived in Edmonds, I was sick. My health was bad. My sinuses and my allergies were giving me problems because of the rain I had to leave. I didn't know where to go! All of the states I have lived, Washington had the best fish and sea food.

Chapter XIII

Gambling Syndicate

(1985 – 1986)

Later in 1985, I was living in Sparks, Nevada. When Mr. Al Jones called me up and wanted to talk to me. I asked him "is anything wrong?" He replied "no, I got a business deal for you. Can you meet me tomorrow in Colma at 435 F St.?" I stated, "Yes, is two o'clock okay?" Mr. Jones replied "I'll see you at two o'clock." After he hung up I knew what he wanted! I knew Al about five years and he is an honest man and he is very reliable.

The next day I took the airplane back to San Francisco. Stu Linder, my property manager, picked me up at the airport. Al Jones was waiting for me at 435 F St., my parents used to live there! Stu and Al and myself went to the house to talk business. He wanted to rent that house

for bookmaking and offshore betting! This house was special to me. That was my parent's house .I got very emotional. Al could tell I didn't want to rent this house for bookmaking! Al told me he will pay me $3000 per month to rent this house. I replied" you pay the rent, which is $800 per month and then you can give me a deposit of $2000 cash per month." Al agreed, saying "can I move in tomorrow?" Naturally, I said "yes, you can."Stu drove me back to the airport. When I arrived in Sparks, Nevada, same old thing, gambling and women.

In 1985, I didn't have a lot of money because the estate was still in probate. It took about six months for me to become the owner of the estate.

There was no one to dispute the estate. So I own the properties, stocks and the money in the bank

To the reader, let's go back two years. I would like to share this **mystery** with you. Two puzzling **events** that occurred before my parents died. Both happened at 435 F St. in, Colma! Today, I'm trying not to think about what happened. It's a mystery of my dark past this is so bizarre. I know **the reader** is not going to believe this, but I assure you this did happen to me. **Are you with me**?

In 1983, my mother was dying in a convalescent home. Later in 1984 on father was also dying in a convalescent home. In October of 1983, I went to 435 F St., (yes that's the same house the gambling syndicate lived in 1985), to see if my parents left any valuable items. I opened all the doors in the front room also in the dining room. I didn't see anything of great value. I then went in the kitchen I opened all the doors and found nothing.

I was looking at the gas stove, it was an old-fashioned stove, I opened the door of the stove and I saw a brown box. What the hell is a brown box doing in the stove! I immediately took the box out and opened it. There were all one hundred dollar bills, all wrapped with a rubber band! I was in shock and out of my mind. My body was paralyzed I just couldn't speak! There were 20 stacks of $100 bills. I started to count the money, I had to stop. I was sweating and getting very nervous. I was thinking, what is all this money doing in my parents stove? I finished counting the money there was 100,000 in that stove! Where do I put this money! I can't put it in the bank the IRS will ask me where I got the money. I'm in trouble.

I put all the money in my safe deposit box in the Bank of America. My mother was on a respirator I father is out of his mind! I have $100,000 I found in a gas stove. Can you imagine how fucked up I was? After my mother died, my father's mental health got worse. You never knew that his wife died, but he didn't want to live anymore. He lost a lot of weight and they had to amputate his leg.

In July 1984, one month before my father died, I went to see him in the convalescent home, he looked awful. He was calling for my mother I told him she is in the other room. It was terrible. I was crying! He must've weighed 80 pounds! He couldn't live without my mother. That is real love. He signaled me to come closer. He then whispered something in my year. I could barely hear him, I heard him say very softly "look, trap door" I couldn't understand him, dad say it again. He repeated it again "look ,trap door." I still didn't know what he meant. I knew his mind was going. I told him I will see him tomorrow. I couldn't look at him anymore, it was killing me!

When I got home, I was cursing God for keeping my father alive. I went straight to 435 F St. to look at my father's gun room. It was in the garage. The gun room was locked, but I have all the keys of 435 F St., so there was no problem. When I was in the gun room, it always gets me frightened. I saw all my father's guns. There must've been about 100 guns rifles and shotguns! All those guns are going to be mine. What the hell, am I going to do with them?

This place gives me bad memories. I started to cry, it was so depressing to me! I started to leave, and I remembered my father mentioned the trap door! But I knew my father's mind is going! He doesn't know who or where he is. Anyway, I didn't know what made me do this. I just picked up the carpet, to get to the trap door.(remember that's where the machine gun was) I pulled up, to open the trap door and I looked in. I saw four boxes of bullets and then I saw a miniature safe next to the other boxes. It wasn't heavy, so I lifted it up and place it on the floor. I tried to open the safe, it was unlocked. I was scared to look inside, but I did anyway. I couldn't believe what I saw. I was yelling "Oh my God." There were stacks of one hundred dollar bills in the miniature safe. I was thinking about the money I saw in the stove. I immediately closed the door of the gun room. I was sweating, now I'm afraid this money doesn't belong to my father. I got one of my father's shotgun loaded it, and was ready if someone was watching me. Then I started to count the money. There were **400,000**, all in one hundred dollar bill. Why did my father had **$500,000** in his house. My father never sold any drug and never was involved with any bookie. In fact, he hated gambling, that's why he hated me.

The next day I put all the money in my safe deposit box at the Bank of America. I had half of the million dollars in the safe deposit box. To this day, I always think of where that money came from! **There is only one answer**. My father had many properties, no mortgage on any of them. He had money in the banks and in stocks and bonds. There is no reason for my father to have all this money is his house. So, the money my father had, in the house was **Mob Money**. My father had to be holding the money for someone connected with my mob. Also I knew he was **connected** to the **mob.**

Now, I knew why the mob, left Colma in 1975. I know why they never killed me! I believe my father stopped them from **killing me**! There were a lot the rumors about the Mayor of San Francisco Joe Alioto, that he was **associated with the mob**. Joe Alioto was a **very close friend** of my father.

Let's get back to 1986, I moved from Sparks, Nevada to Reno, Nevada. I got a phone call from Stu Linder, in a depressed and a sad voice, he said that for 435 F St. was raided by the FBI. Also he told me everybody in the house got arrested. I didn't know what to say! Stu told me the FBI wanted to talk to me. I was shocked, but I knew this was going to happen. The gambling syndicate was making a lot of money, and they were one of the biggest bookmakers in the San Francisco area. They also had offshore betting. Many of them were betting large amounts of money. I knew what they were doing, but I didn't care. I never placed a bet with them. I never got involved in their operations!

The next day, I took the airplane to San Francisco, Stu picked me up at the airport, he looked very nervous. I told him everything will be okay, don't worry. I rented a house to Al Jones. Do not worry about the FBI, they got nothing on me! Stu's driving was erratic. I told him to pull over so we could talk. I told Stu how is the FBI going to prove that I knew Al Jones was a bookmaker. What is the fuck is wrong with you? Stu started to cry. I said, "Get out of the car, and let me drive." I got back on the roadway I was going north on Hillside Boulevard, heading toward Colma. The appointment that Stu made with the FBI agent was at one o'clock.

I had an hour to calm Stu down. I tried to tell him that he would not be interrogated. Just keep your mouth shut. If you don't we are both in trouble. Don't you know that? You fucking wimp. When I got to Colma, I parked the car at 435 F St., there were two FBI agents waiting for me. They both asked me a lot of questions. I told them I knew nothing about the bookmakers. I just rented the house to Mr. Jones. One of the agents asked me if I knew Al Jones. I replied "No, I don't." I said, "the only time I see him is when he pays me the rent." The FBI agent could not prove that I was involved with the gambling operation, but **they knew I was lying**. After the FBI agents left, I told Stu to have 435 F St. cleaned and up the rent from "$800 to $900" per month. I always had a lot of respect for the FBI. They don't fuck around, they keep coming after you. Nothing bothered me then! I had a lot of money. **I wasn't scared of anybody**.

Later that day, I was approached by a friend, Billy Ringo. He was one of the individual that got arrested at 435 F St. He asked me, "would you take this money and keep it for me." I asked him how much? He replied

"$30,000." I knew he was hiding the money from the FBI. I didn't care. I took the $30,000. Three months later, I gave him all the money back!

The next day, I returned to Reno. I was thinking what an idiot Mr. Jones was! Later on, I was told that someone ratted on Mr. Jones. It probably was someone who was betting with Jones and lost a lot of money. Al Jones lost millions of dollars, because he trusted everyone.

A few years later, Al Jones died. It was a sad day for me. He was a friendly and generous person.

Chapter XIV

Documentary Movie

(1985 – 1989)

In 1985, Mr. Barry Brann paged me at the MGM casino, I knew him from Colma. He was a director from Los Angeles, California. We went to the coffee shop to talk about filming a documentary movie about my political career. He was interested in all the ups and downs in my life. Barry knew I got arrested for vote fraud in 1976 and then the miracle comeback in 1980. It was in 1980, when I won the Colma election and make California's history.

I told Barry that I wasn't interested in making a documentary movie about me. It would bring back horrible memories. I just couldn't do it. I knew Barry was disappointed, and I told him I am sorry. Barry gave me his phone number and told me if I change my mind, to call him. When Barry left, I knew he was mad at me. But the memory of my parent's death is too much for me to deal with. I can't go through that anymore!

Three months later, Barry Brann came back to the MGM casino. The next day, he found me at the sport casino. This time he begged me to do the documentary movie. I've been losing a lot of money gambling, so I gave in and told him, "I will do it." Barry was astonished. He was so happy, he said, "When I get back to San Francisco, I'll call you!" I told him I was taking acting lessons in Studio City, California. At that time, I was living in Sparks, Nevada and in Los Angeles, California. I told Barry let's hurry up and do this documentary movie

Two weeks later, Barry called me and said he was coming to Reno, tomorrow! He wanted to tell me his plan of how and where he's going to film. Also he told me the documentary film would take about 28 min. It will take about a year before the documentary is finished. I was shocked, why does it take a year to do a 20 minutes film. Barry explained to me, first I have to get a crew. Then he wanted to hire a helicopter, so he could film Colma from different directions. Also Barry had to film in different cities, places and get opinions from people in Colma. Barry likes the fact I was arrested in 1976 and then I got elected in 1980! I asked him what cities you are going to film in? Barry said, Colma, Golden Gate racetrack, in Albany, California. We will finish filming in Reno, Nevada. Barry said, "When I finish filming, I have to do the editing, that will take six months or more." I told him I'm going to enjoy doing this movie because this will keep me away from gambling.

Two weeks later, Barry and his crew started filming at the Colma Town Hall. I had to get permission to film at the Town Hall. There was no problem, remember I was still a councilman of Colma. After the filming, I was going to resign as councilman.

We went to Golden Gate Fields racetrack to film my horses. Barry met my trainer, Dale Steward, a well-known cowboy. After we left the racetrack, we went to Reno, Nevada. I was driving my famous car, the ExCalibur. I love that car, even if it looks like a Pimp Mobile. The filming was over. It was fun. Barry had to get permission to play three songs in the movie. The singers were **Simon and Garfunkel, Conway Twitty and Wayne Newton.** I wanted Barry to tell about my involvement with the Zodiac killer. Barry was a very conservative person. When I mentioned the Zodiac killer, he was afraid.

The documentary movie was called "**The King of Colma.**" In 1986 to 1988 "The King of Colma," was shown in **six States** and **Canada**.

"The King of Colma" played at the Bally's theater. Reno, Nevada. The first person, who came in was **Mayor of Reno**, Pete Sferrazza. Following him was the famous Joe Conforte. Naturally, he came in with two women. He was the owner of the famous brothel, "**The Mustang Ranch.**"

In 1989, the movie was **nominated** for an **Academy Award**. It didn't win!

Lets get back to 1985. Finally I resigned from the Town Council in Colma. No one will ever accomplish what I did in politics. I was in politics for 12 years. In **1964** and **1968**, I made **California history**.

In the **State of California**, no councilman has ever made a political comeback after he got **arrested** for **Vote Fraud**! **In1980,** my famous comeback, made **California history again!**

In October of 1989, page 15 of the famous movie newspaper "Variety". My picture took up the entire page! It was a honor, for my documentary movie, to appear in that famous newspaper! I can not explain in words how I felt! That day, everyone will remember the small town of Colma! My parents would be proud of me! I know many people were jealous of what I had accomplished! My documentary movie was nominated for an Academy Award! To the reader, Before I became the "Cowboy", I was already famous!

Chapter XV

Tragedy

"Cowboy" (1990 – 1996)

In 1990, I'm still living in Edmunds, Washington. When I got a phone call from my insurance agent. He told me that 421 F St. burned down. I was in such shock it took me two minutes to catch my breath. (That was the house I lived in with Linda, my second wife.) The agent told me a tenant got seriously injured. The tenant got third-degree burns on his face. After talking to the agent, I was so depressed I couldn't talk anymore. I told him I will see you tomorrow.

The next day, I took the airplane to San Francisco and then I took a cab to Colma. When I saw what was left of the house, made me sick to my stomach. I was sued for $2 million, and I was assured for only 1 million dollars. That would be a major problem. Anyway, the injured person settled for $1 million.

Last year, the earthquake caused me a lot of money. Then I ended up losing $400,000 on this house. The town of Colma pronounced that the house was condemned. I had the house demolished. I was in tears, that cost me $50,000. I don't know what was going to happen next, but I had enough! I hate everybody. I was using abusive language, and I hated "God." I was disgusted, the only thing I could think of, was I'm getting punished for what I did in Lake Tahoe

I took the plane back to Washington. The next week I moved to Reno. I drove the ExCalibur. My friend David, who flew in from Reno, was with me. I had the Rolls Royce transported to Reno. When I got to Reno, I was so depressed. One week later, the Rolls arrived. I didn't bet like I did in the 1980's, but I was still betting $50,000 a week. I mortgage more houses and was losing money as quickly as I got it

Later in 1990, I was staying at Bally's casino. I was in a suite, naturally it was free. All the dealers and pit bosses were saying, "The "Cowboy" is back! I parked the ExCalibur and the Rolls Royce in Valet parking.

I came back, after I had been away over a year. The earthquake hurt me bad and losing that house was a disaster. I was the "**Cowboy**." Did I stop my large bets. Fuck No! My reputation killed me. I had to make large bets. Don't get me wrong, I didn't have to keep my reputation. I was a big gambler anyway!

After the earthquake, I was never the same. **To the reader**, if you are a **crazy individual**, you will enjoy the bizarre events that happened in 1990 through 1992.

The next ten months, I stayed at Bally's casino was frightening. I was still losing $50,000 a week. I couldn't win! I was flipping a coin, to see what team I was going to bet on, and I still lost! Jack called me a pathetic gambler. I was a violent person, but I didn't take my anger out on people. I busted a total of five television sets in my hotel room. Every time, I busted a television set, Bally's gave me another one. At one time, I had three television sets in my room. Bally's didn't care what damage I did as long as I kept betting.

To keep me away from gambling I went to brothels. Many times I drove to Carson City Nevada. There were to brothels, that I patronize most of the time. The brothels were located in a culdesac. The names of the brothels were Kit Kat and Kitty's. I met a prostitute at the Kit Kat her name was Windy, she gave me a massage. She was fun to talk to. All prostitutes are fucked up. Usually they are on drugs and they have a pimp! I hated pimps, they are bloodsucking parasites.

A week later I met Windy at Bally's casino. We had lunch at the coffee shop. I knew she liked me, but I stayed away from prostitutes! We went up to my hotel room and she gave me a massage. She didn't charge me, that was nice of her. She asked me if I had a girlfriend. I replied "no I don't." I was fucking many girls, but I didn't have a girlfriend. Anyway, she was leaving for Las Vegas, that's where she lives.

Let's get to the exciting things that happened in 1990. One night I was watching a baseball game in my room. I bet on the St. Louis Cardinals against the Chicago Cubs. I bet $9000 to win $8000. That means, if I win,

I get back $17,000. When I make a bet on a football or baseball game, I am a different person. I am totally fucked up. I don't sit down, I pace back and forth like a fucken animal!

That night I was losing 5 to 1 going into the ninth inning. I was fucked again. I was so mad I had to leave or I would break another television set. I took the sport ticket and placed it in the toilet and **urinated on it**! I left and took the elevator down to the casino. I was walking around the blackjack tables when I came to the Crap game. I saw Fred, a friend of mine, He was playing craps. I came over to him and before I could say a word, Fred said,"Did you bet the baseball game tonight?" I replied, "Yes I did, and I took the fucking Cardinals." Immediately, Fred said, "the game is in extra innings tied up at 5 to 5!". I was stunned. I told Fred, I bet on the Cardinals, and my ticket is in the toilet.

I quickly walked to the elevator and took it up to my room. When I got there I opened the door and rushed to the bathroom. I got the ticket out of the toilet. Thank God, I never flushed the toilet. I immediately turned on the television set and put on the baseball game. The game was in the last of the tenth inning still tied at 5 to 5. I was watching the game, and drying the ticket with my handheld dryer. The Cardinals scored a run in the tenth inning to win 6 to 5. I was jumping up and down like a lunatic! I finished drying the ticket, but it still **smelled like urine**. I sprayed Cologne on the ticket; the odor of urine was still on the ticket. I was so embarrassed to cash the ticket, but then I thought about the $17,000, that changed my mind. I left and took the elevator down to the casino.

When I got to the cashier's cage, Jim came over to me and said, "You finally won a game!" He took my crumbled ticket and tried to put it in the machine, it wouldn't go in. He started to read the numbers on the ticket. He looked at me and said, "Cowboy, this ticket smells of urine!" I was speechless. Jim said, "Oh my God, you pissed on this ticket." He called the manager of the of the cashier department to verify the ticket. I started to laugh, and I couldn't stop. Jim told the manager, "Cowboy pissed on this ticket, I'm not touching this ticket." The manager was staring at me. I smiled and said, "Give me my fucking money!" The manager went back and got a pair of gloves. He picked up the ticket put it in the machine. He was very mad! But he knew I was the Cowboy! So he can do nothing about it. He gave me $17,000 all in hundreds. He told me Cowboy, please never do that again. I stared at him saying ,"Fuck You, nobody tells me what to do." Then I walked away! I knew I was wrong but that's the way I was. I was betting and losing, **millions of dollars at Bally's casino**. I could do anything I wanted and no one stopped me.

To the reader, From 1986 – 1992, No one had more power than the Cowboy! You don't believe me. You think I'm making this up? Just keep reading! **The Cowboy was a legend of his time.** Let me tell you what happened two months later. It was a Saturday afternoon and I was in my hotel room watching the college football game between Florida State and Miami. I bet $50,000 on Florida State. When I bet a large sum of money on a game I'm in my own world. I always watch the game by myself. Remember, I'm a violent gambler, but I only break television sets. There is less than a minute left in the fourth quarter of the football game. Florida State is losing by two points. Florida State is trying to kick a field goal to win the game. It was a short field goal. I'm counting my money. The kicker for Florida State fucks up and missed the field goal! Miami wins the game. **I lost $50,000**, what a way to lose. I was so fucked up, I broke the screen on the television set. Just another normal day!

I left the hotel room, heading for the elevator. I saw a security guard coming toward me. I knew all the security guards, this particular security guard hated me. When the security guard came closer to me he said, "Hey Cowboy, how much did you lose?" I remember I was in a very bad mood. I replied, "None of your fucken business!" The security guard said "That no way to talk to me!" I just totally lost it, I said, "I'm sick of you, get the fuck out of my way." He tried to **stop me** from passing him, also he grabbed me. I **slapped him** in the face and he immediately called for help with his radio.

Three security guards came to assist him. One of the security guard was dressed in a suit. He was the boss of all the security. He grabbed me and walked me to my room. He asked me "What happened Cowboy?" I told him what happened , and he said "stay in my room, I would be back in an hour." Finally, he came to see me, as he walked in my hotel room he saw the broken television set. He was laughing so much, he had to sit down. He called Bob ,(he was boss of the sports casino) and he told me everything will be okay. The security guard told me, the guard that grabbed you will be fired. Before he left he said, "I'll have someone come to your room and take away the broken television set. You want another television?" I smiled at him and said "Yes, get me two more." The only thing I could think of was, I'm glad this fucking day is over. That night I couldn't sleep I was thinking about the security guard that was going to be fired.

The next day, I did something unusual. All the money I was losing and memories of the earthquake were getting to me. I left my hotel room, and immediately went straight to the office where Bob worked. Bob was a powerful man, he could do anything. I walked in like I owned the place. I'm the Cowboy! Bally's wants my action, so I can do anything I want. Bob was with someone, but I don't care. The told the secretary, "when Bob is finished talking, tell him the Cowboy wants to talk to him.

When Bob was finished with that customer, he called me in. Bob is from New York, you know what that means, he takes no shit from nobody. I told him, I am losing every fucken game, but I know you already know that. Bob stated every week he gets a list of all the games I bet. I need a favor Bob. You've heard about what happened with me and the security guard. Bob said "I did and I will take care of it!" Thank you Bob, I feel bad about what is going to happen to the security guard. Do me a favor and **don't fire him**! I provoked him! Bob replied "are you lying to me!" I smiled and said "yes I'm lying, but he has a family, and I would feel bad if he got fired. Bob said, okay, Cowboy, "I'll give him another chance!" The Cowboy could do anything. **To the reader**, how many gamblers do you know, that could stop the **Security Guard** from **getting fired**! How many customers do you know that have the power to do that? **None**!

You would think all the excitement of the Cowboy would finally end, but it continues, with tragic endings! Money and women, where the downfall of the Cowboy! And the downfall of many men. The Cowboy never stopped betting large sums of money! It is amazing! That's why he was famous. It wasn't the sickness of gambling that destroyed him, he just didn't care. He didn't want to die being rich!

In 1991 the Cowboy had three girlfriends. Not only does he have major gambling problems he also has his girlfriends to deal with. This has to end up in a tragedy, and it did! I'm going to tell you about the women in "Cowboy" life that ended in **death**. All his problems were self-induced. But he tried to help women. That was his demise! Remember, I'm talking about myself! I don't want to write about the Cowboy anymore. I'm getting sick to my stomach. I owe it **to the reader** to continue.

Before the Cowboy came to Reno, he was married three times. All his relationships with women were one on one! After he got the money, fancy cars, and the wild women of Reno. The Cowboy became a **male whore**!

In 1991, I left Bally's and rented a house in Reno. The cowboy was dating three women and fucking two blackjack dealers. Also I was still losing a lot of money gambling.

A horrible event happened at Bally's. Jack and I were eating at the steak house, when Windy came to see me. She found out that I was fucking the waitress, who was working at the steak house. When sat down right next to Jack, she didn't say a word to me. I knew something was wrong. To make things worse, Betty was my waitress. Windy got up and was looking for Betty. I immediately got up and grabbed Wendy, I was trying to escort her out of the restaurant. Betty came over to me, thinking that something is wrong.(Betty doesn't know I'm dating Windy)

I didn't know what to do! Windy was trying to hit Betty, I quickly grabbed Windy, so Betty could get away. Betty went outside the restaurant, Wendy followed her out. I got in between Windy and Betty trying to break it up. Windy turned and kicked me in the leg. I grabbed her and then she slapped me on the face. She was crying! Thank God, two security guards arrived and grabbed Wendy. One of the security guards asked me "What is going on Cowboy!" I replied, "Everything is under control." Windy was still crying, and calling me dirty names. I told the security guards to leave her go. Usually, the security guards never go against me. Finally, Windy left the casino. I knew sooner or later, I was going to get caught. I turned to the security guards and shook their hands, giving them one hundred dollars each.

After that day, I had enough. I can't go on dating all these women! So, I stopped dating. It was all my fault, I hated myself. I had to do one more thing.

Two day, went by then I went to the Kit Kat brothel in Carson City. I took Jack with me. I was hoping to find Windy. I don't know how I done it, but I got her out of the brothel. I took Jack home and then I took Windy to my house in Reno. She called her daughter, who lived in Las Vegas and told her she will be coming home tomorrow. Windy's daughter sometimes lives with her ex-boyfriend, who is involved **with the mob**. What a **fucked up situation** .

I told Windy, "Is he the father of your kid?" She replied, "Yes he is!" I was yelling at her saying, "If he is involved with the mob, your life could be in danger." She replied "he wouldn't hurt me." I was so fucking mad, I was screaming at her. I said, **"He is not going to lose his daughter. You will be buried in the desert!**

I couldn't sleep that night, bad thoughts were going through my mind. If he knew she was coming to live with me, my life could be in danger too!

The next day, I was going to take her to the airport, but she insisted on taking a cab. When she got in the cab, I told her to call me when she gets to Las Vegas. I had a bad feeling that **I would never see her again**!

Later in 1991, I still haven't heard from Windy. I was getting worried. Finally, she called me and said everything is okay. Windy told me she is moving to Reno and bringing her daughter with her. After she told me that, I broke out in a sweat. I asked her, "Did you tell your ex-boyfriend that you are moving to Reno?"

She replied, "Yes I did." In a soft spoken voice, I said to her, "Does he know you are taking your daughter with you?" She replied, "Yes why are you asking me that. I would never leave my daughter in Las Vegas." I was begging her not to come to Reno. Please! Listen to me. I will come to Las Vegas in a limousine; I will bring two bodyguards with me." I told Windy you don't understand, you fucken idiot. You are in danger! I will have my **UZI, a submachine gun,** in a suitcase. The UZI, it's a deadly assault weapon. Windy said, "I will see you next week!" Then she hung up the phone. I was scared. I knew she will never leave **Las Vegas alive**!

Two months goes by, Wendy didn't call me, she just disappeared. Jack and I went to the brothels in Carson City. No one saw or heard from Windy. I didn't want to think that **she was murdered**.

One month later, Wendy is still missing. There is nothing I can do but hope and pray. I said, over and over, "Someone is going to pay for killing Windy. That mother fucker must die. But **who is he! Where is he**!

In 1992, I sold the Excalibur to a Japanese man for $30,000. I was so sad. I did want to sell, but I was thinking of moving out of Nevada.

Two months later, I left the house and moved in with Jack. He was living in a trailer. I was so fucked up, thinking about Windy. I did everything in my power to save her from getting murdered. I guess it was destiny. I tried to make myself think, she ran away with her daughter. I remember telling Jack that fucking ex-boyfriend got away with **murder**. Windy was **buried like an animal**! No one deserves to die like that.

Something bothers me! I am afraid **the reader** doesn't believe me. I didn't **kill Windy**! I got a strange feeling that **the reader** is thinking that. I am sorry I should not have said that. I guess I'm getting **paranoid**!

After what happened to Windy, I was betting large sums of money gambling. Naturally, I was losing, but I guess I didn't care anymore.

To the reader, I felt awful about writing this paragraph. I had to stop many times. It was so intense and extremely emotional. It brought back terrible memories!

Later in 1992, I got a phone call from the Las Vegas Police Department.

They must have got Jack's phone number from the brothel in Carson City. A female detective asked me, "Can I speak to the Cowboy?" I said, I'm the "Cowboy." The detective said, "What is your name?" I replied, "My name is Raymond Ottoboni." She asked me "Do you know why I am calling you?" I started to stutter and then I said, "Yes, this is about Windy, is she still missing?" The detective replied in a loud voice, "How did you know she was missing?"(The detective mentioned her real name, Windy was her nickname. I don't remember her real name) I told the detective, Windy was moving to Reno with her daughter.

The detective asked me if I have been to Las Vegas last year. She also specified the month of May. (Windy disappeared in May of 1991) I told her, I've been in Reno for the past two years. My roommate, Jack is my witness. I totally lost it. I had enough of this bullshit! In an angry tone of voice, I said, "I know who killed Windy and so does the Las Vegas Police Department. **Why are you calling me?**"

The detective was getting mad, and said angrily, "I thought you could help us!" I took a deep breath and calmly said, "I am an ex-cop from a small town in California. **I know who killed Windy and I know she is buried in the Las Vegas desert**! How come the Las Vegas police doesn't know that? Did the Vegas police interrogate Windy's ex-boyfriend? The detective stated "We did, but he had an alibi." I was so fucking mad, I could scream. I replied, The ex-boyfriend paid someone else to kill Windy, and she was buried in the desert you want me to come to Las Vegas to solve the crime? The detective hung up on me! I know the **Las Vegas Police Department doesn't care about finding Windy's killer. They knew she was a prostitute.**

I told Jack if he wanted to go to Las Vegas it would take me a week to kill that mother fucker! Jack replied "do you know his name?" I said "no I don't, but I will find out!" Jack was scared, because Wendy's ex-boyfriend was involved with the mob! Anyway, we didn't go to Las Vegas. Jack never knew about my involvement with the mob back in 1972.

I still had money, I was thinking of killing that fucker, and bury him in the desert just like he had done to Windy.

When I was a cop in 1970, I was a pussycat. In 1992, I could have killed anybody, the money I was losing made me more fucking crazy! You think I'm just talking bull shit! Yes, I am talking to **you the reader**, the Cowboy **never quits!** Just keep reading I'm not **finished just yet.**

The next night, Jack and I went to Carson City. I told Jack, what I was going to do to help Windy. Jack didn't like my idea. I was looking for a particular person that maybe could help me. When we got to Kitty's that is another brothel next to the Kit Kat, I looked for him and he wasn't there. Jack and I had been in Kitty's before, all the brothels are the same. I was hoping to see a person, they called the mountain man! He's a regular customer at Kitty's. I was so fucking mad, that he wasn't there.

I told Jack I was going to get a massage, if a big man with a cowboy hat comes in tell him I want to see him. Jack replied "how big is he?" I shook my head and replied is about 6'5" and has an ugly beard. He looks like a mountain man! After I got the massage, I went to the front room. Jack was talking to a prostitute. I knew most of the girls didn't like me, because they knew I hated prostitutes. Yes, I know what's going through your mind. Windy was a prostitute. Windy was different, she was a classy girl, you would never know she was a prostitute. She was always scared of her ex-boyfriend. I guess I just felt sorry for Windy. Anyway, guess who came in the brothel? I was so happy to see the mountain man. He came and sat on the couch. He never talked to anybody. This is not going to be easy. Jack looked at me and said "Cowboy what are you going to do?" Jack could see the mountain man was a weird person.

I remember the manager of the brothel telling me that the mountain man is a miner. I approached the mountain man, he was still sitting on the couch, and I told him "I need your help." He stared at me and didn't say a word. I knew this wasn't going to be easy. But I knew money buys everybody. I knew I had to be calm throughout the conversation with this person. I came right to the point. "Let's go outside, and see if you can help me, I'll give you $5000!" His eyes were wide open and he made a motion to me, that he would follow me outside. Still he hasn't spoken a single word. What a fucken weirdo.

When we got outside I was shocked, he said to me "can I help you?" I asked "you have a name?" He replied "I don't tell anyone my name." I shook my head and said let's forget the names. I know you work in a mine. I need for you to show me how to make a bomb! I know you must have a permit to buy dynamite. The mountain man replied "what are you going to do with the dynamite?" I came closer to him and said "what do you care, you are getting $5000, and no one will know you gave the dynamite to me. What the fuck would you care what I do with it?" This person is so fucked up I'm yelling at him, and he just looks at me with those crazy eyes. He smiled at me and said "I know what you are going to do and I don't care. But I want $10,000!" I told him "that's a lot of money."

He pointed to my fancy car and said $10,000 is nothing to you, that's one sport bet!" I said "how the hell do you know that?" The mountain man replied "the Cowboy is famous, you have lost millions of dollars." I guess I had no choice. I told him "you win I'll pay you $10,000. Now, I want to see you make the bomb. Is that a problem? "The mountain man said "meet me here at two o'clock tomorrow afternoon." I told him I'll see you tomorrow. I went in Kitty's and got Jack and we went back to Reno Jack asked me, is he going to make the bomb? I said "yes I am going to meet him tomorrow afternoon." Jack looked uneasy, something was wrong. I asked him "Jack are you okay?" Jack always spoke slowly, but this time his voice was different.

In an angry tone he said "Cowboy, please don't do this. It is a federal offense having a bomb. No matter what you do Cowboy, you can bring Windy back." Jack started to cry, I've known Jack for eight years, and I never saw him cry. Jack was like a father to me, seeing him cry affected me. I pulled over off the roadway and promised Jack I wouldn't go to Las Vegas, but I wanted to see how a bomb is made. Naturally, I was lying to him! Jack didn't say another word until we got to Reno.

We went straight to the Peppermill Casino. Jack told me he was sorry for the way he acted. I told Jack no one gives a fuck about Windy's death. **She died like a dog**! If I go to Las Vegas that fucker, that killed Windy is dead! You know how many guns I have, and how crazy I am. But, I gave you my word, that I will not go to Vegas. Let's not talk about this anymore!

The next day, I drove the Rolls-Royce to Carson City. I had a two o'clock appointment with the mountain man. I arrived at Kitty's before two o'clock, I'm always on time. I knew the mountain man wouldn't let me down, especially for $10,000. Many thoughts were going through my mind, I wonder if I'm being set up! Here comes the mountain man driving that dirty old car. I got out of my car and he signaled me to follow him.

I got back in the Rolls and I followed him. I was not familiar with Carson City. When he was driving on the dirt roads, I was totally lost. He stopped next to an old broken down house. I got out of the car, and he told me to wait. I said to myself "what the fuck am I doing here?" He came out of his house and went into the garage. I just stood there like a jackass! I had diamonds on my fingers, driving a Rolls and now I'm here with a crazy fucker in the boondocks!

The mountain man came out with a round plastic jar and a tiny bottle. He told me to watch what he was doing and stand still. I saw him insert a yellow liquid in the plastic jar. He added another liquid to the jar. I asked him what is that yellow liquid? He said "that is **nitroglycerin!**" When I added the other liquid it becomes dynamite, if I drop this both of us would be dead. He put a lid over the jar. He said "it's all ready to go." I asked him to show me how to put the bomb underneath the car so it would explode. We both got under his car and he showed me where to put the bomb. He put the bomb on top of the exhaust pipe. Then he applied a sticky clay that was molded onto the exhaust pipe. He told me when the exhaust pipe gets hot it will ignite the bomb. I was amazed by what he told me.

Something bothered me, I told the mountain man before I give you the money I have to see if the bomb works. He stated "I understand, come with me." I got in his broken down car and he took me towards the mountain's. We stopped and I saw an old car out in the wilderness. He took the dynamite out of his trunk and put it under the old car I asked him "did you put it on top of the exhaust pipe?" He replied "yes." He started the old car, and then got out of the car, grabbed me and we started to walk away from the car.

We walked about a half a block, He told me it would blow up sooner if someone was driving the car. I don't remember how long it took when it exploded. If there was a man in that old car he would be blown to pieces! He asked me if I was satisfied? I replied "Yes I am." I told him to keep the bomb for me. I don't know where to keep it. If I don't come back you can keep it. I paid him **$10,000** in hundred dollar bills! When we got back to the car I followed him back to the main street. He told me to go north. I never came back to get the bomb. Maybe someday I will find him if he is still alive.

Two months later I had horrible dreams about Windy. I was thinking of going to Las Vegas. **I knew getting that bomb was a terrible idea!** My main concern was how I was going to find that fucken murderer. A thought came to my mind, maybe Rico could help me. Rico lives in Sacramento, California.

The next day I told Jack I was going to Sacramento. I'll be back the next day. I didn't want to drive the Rolls so I rented a car. I already notified Rico that I was coming to see him.

I arrived at Rico's house about two o'clock in the afternoon. I was scared to tell him about my problem. I told him what I needed Rico said he knew of someone that could help me I was amazed. There is still a chance to get that person who killed Windy. The bomb was a good idea, but it would cause me many problems. This device is a killing machine. By now **the reader** knows that I am in the process of committing a crime. I hope

the reader doesn't hate me. I'm doing everything I can to find Windy's killer!

The next day I met Rico's friend Ben, he didn't talk much, but that was good because he never asked me any questions. I asked him could you put a pistol (UZI) in any briefcase? He replied "yes I can it will cost you $2000!" I told him that's no problem I also told him I already have the briefcase and the pistol.

To the reader I hope you are not confused. The excitement is about to **explode**! Let me start by telling you that Ben is a California Highway Patrolman, **are you shocked**?

I went back to Reno and in a week Rico called me to come back to Sacramento. He told me to bring the briefcase and the pistol.

I left the next day, I drove the Rolls and was very nervous. When I got to Sacramento, I wanted to turn back, but I continued on. When I got to Rico's house, Ben was already there. I gave him my brown briefcase, and the pistol (UZI). He looks and acted like a professional, also he wore gloves. He told me Rico will call me when the briefcase is finished. This work could take months. I knew Ben's job wasn't going to be easy. Rico lives in the wilderness, so there will be no problem in shooting the pistol. The next day I went back to Reno.

A month later, I got a call from Rico. He told me the job is finished. I said "I'll see you tomorrow, is two o'clock in the afternoon okay?" Rico replied "I will see you then."

I drove to Sacramento and I was scared. Why is a policeman helping me to commit a murder? I was puzzled, but I knew Rico wouldn't be involved in a **set up** against me. **To the reader**, I know you would go after the person that had murdered your girlfriend! "**Am I right**?"

When I got to Rico's house, many thoughts were going through my mind. When I saw the briefcase, I was amazed how Ben structured the pistol to the briefcase. We all went outside, Rico wanted be the first one to shoot the pistol. He had the briefcase on his right side. One hand holding the briefcase and the other hand on the trigger, which was under the briefcase.

The **briefcase blew up in his arms**. Rico's ribs were bruised. That was horrible; Ben and I were in shock. The briefcase was torn apart. Ben looked at the briefcase; the pistol was still inside the briefcase. He told me there was no ventilation in the briefcase. There was too much smoke coming out of the briefcase; also the noise of the pistol had to be corrected. Ben told me to get another briefcase. He would be coming to Reno next weekend.

Ben called me on Friday, from the Peppermill Casino. He was with his wife. Naturally, his wife wasn't aware that Ben was making a briefcase for me. Especially, a briefcase that would kill someone. Anyway, I gave him the reddish brown briefcase to Ben. The briefcase looked very elegant, no one would ever think there is a pistol in it. Ben left the next day. He told me he would call me in a month.

Later, I got a phone call from Ben. He told me the briefcase is finished. The waiting was over, I was very happy to hear it.

This is the third time I went to Sacramento, California and hoping this is the last time. I finally told Jack what I was doing. Jack said, "You are out of your mind." He told me over and over you can't bring Windy back! I replied, "I have to do this!"

The next day, I drove to Sacramento, California. I got there in the afternoon; Rico and Ben were waiting for me. I was so excited, that I had to take a tranquilizer, to calm me down. We went outside and Rico was again the first to shoot the pistol from inside the briefcase. Rico, (wearing gloves) was aiming at the target. He fired the pistol, **all eight shots hit the target**. Ben put a screen to cover the holes in the briefcase. He covered the inside of the briefcase with a sheet of foil. There was hardly any noise or smoke coming out from the briefcase. All the casings were in the briefcase. It was my turn to test the pistol, it felt uncomfortable. **All six shots hit the target**. Ben corrected all his mistakes. I was satisfied; it was a **perfect killing machine**. The briefcase looked like any normal briefcase. There were two holes in the briefcase, one for the trigger and the other one for the barrel of the gun. All holes were covered up by snap locks, before shooting you must turn the briefcase around. **That was a professional job**. I paid Ben **$2000** and gave Rico **$500**. Rico wished me good luck in Las Vegas. I said "Thank you, I will need it!"

The next day, I went back to Reno. I accomplished what I set out to do.

One month later, I rented a car and headed for Las Vegas. The briefcase was in the trunk. When I got to Las Vegas, I went looking for Windy's house. I already knew that was going to be my biggest problem. I had to be careful of my driving. If a Las Vegas police officer stops me and happens to search the trunk, I would be arrested.

A week later and I'm totally lost. I searched everywhere but I couldn't find Windy's house. I thought of going to the Las Vegas police. They gave me Windy's boyfriend's name and he gets killed I would be wanted for murder. I did this all for nothing!

The next day I drove back to Reno I was very depressed. The murder of Windy will never be solved. But I know who did it .**So does the reader!**

In 1993, I met Katie; she was working as a cocktail waitress, at the Hilton casino. She was a lot of fun to be with. She saw me many times, but did not know how to approach me. Matt the bartender, told me that she wanted to go out with me. I dated so many cocktail waitresses and never had too much luck with them. But anyway, I asked Katie if she wanted to go to dinner. She said, "yes when do you want to go?" I replied how about tomorrow night?

She agreed, so we went out to dinner. We had a good time she was very skinny and also had a small baby I should have known something was wrong. I was always stupid when it comes to women on drugs. I dated Katie for a long time and never knew she was a heroin addict. When I found out what she was it was too late. I was in love with her! All the marriages I had and girlfriends I was involved with Katie was the only girl I ever loved. I'm going to make this chapter a short one. I'm sorry, I can't talk much about what happened! I just can't deal with it. **You the reader,** I hope you understand!

In 1994 we got along good. Katie was getting off heroin, but they put Katie on methadone. Sooner or later you have to get off methadone. That is very hard to do. What a fucked up situation! Thank God I don't do any drugs! But my gambling problem is worse than drugs.

Later in 1994, I stopped gambling! Do you believe that! I knew I was going broke, so I had no other choice but to file for bankruptcy. Before I filed, I mortgaged three more houses in Colma. I got $500.00 for the three houses. I put that money in a safe deposit in another state so I can't get to it. My bankruptcy was affecting Katie. I was scared she would go back to drugs. I took her target practicing at a shooting range. She was very good. Katie told me she was a felon. That means she couldn't be around any guns. I noticed Katie was never the same after she couldn't go shooting anymore.

In 1995, I came back from Sacramento, California. My bankruptcy was finished. I was totally broke all the houses were gone. By the bankruptcy rules I was supposed to be totally broke. But **the reader** knows that's not true!

Are you ready! I know you want to read more about killing and how people get away with murder!

In April of 1995, I came home from the casino. I saw Katie cooking I didn't think anything was wrong. I went to the bedroom and started to change clothes. I came directly to the kitchen and asked Katie if she had a good day, she didn't say a word. I knew something was wrong. I figured she was just having a bad day. I went back into the bedroom I didn't know what to do.

I came out and immediately Katie started yelling at me. I said "Katie what's wrong with you?" She came toward me and was very angry! She tried to hit me but she missed. I didn't have enough time to get away from her. I knew she was on drugs, and completely out of her mind. She ran back to the kitchen and came back at me with a kitchen knife. My first reaction was to get my pistol. Quickly, I ran to the bedroom and shut the door. I got my **38 revolver**! I was terrified I didn't want to kill her. I had my shoulder against the door,

Katie was kicking the door trying to get to me! I was so frightened; I didn't want to shoot her! I did something weird. **I unloaded my revolver** and threw it and the cartridges on the bed. I couldn't hold the door anymore. She was still kicking the door, yelling like a maniac, saying I'll kill you! The door was half open, and Katie's knife was coming through the opening! I had to move quickly! I opened the door. She was off balance and I grabbed her hand and pushed upward.

I don't know how I got that knife away from her! She was very strong and being on drugs makes her even stronger! She came back by kicking me with her boot right in the nose. **My nose was bleeding profusely!** As she fell on the floor, I ripped off my shirt pressing into my nose, trying to stop the bleeding. Katie was getting up from the floor, I grabbed her and put her back down on the floor. I was bleeding so bad I couldn't keep her down on the floor.

She immediately ran into the bedroom. I was running after her! Katie took my **38 revolver,** that was on the bed, and pointed it at me. **She pulled the trigger** three or four times. Nothing happened! Remember I already **unloaded** the revolver. Before she knew what happened, I took the revolver away from her, slapping her numerous times in the face. Yelling at her, "that's enough you fucking drug addict." I was covered with blood. **I am a hemophiliac.** When Katie saw all the blood all over my clothes she stopped. If she didn't stop I would have gotten the revolver, loaded it and then I would of killed her!

I drove myself to the hospital in Sparks Nevada. The doctor stopped the bleeding and the nurse gave me a tetanus shot. When I got back to the house, she was sleeping.

The next day, she didn't remember hitting me! I told her I was going to leave. Well, I changed my mind and I gave her another chance. I believe that was the biggest mistake I ever made in my life. The next day she told me that she injected cocaine and heroin into her body! (Speedball) She promised me that this would never happen again!

To the reader, I'm not **finished** yet? There's more **drama** to come! Don't go to the bathroom You don't want to miss this **horrible nightmare!**

On May 12, 1995, I was sitting on the couch watching television, when Katie came home, with her three year old daughter, Niki. Katie was very depressed. She said,"Hi Ray!" Then she went straight in the bedroom and closed the door. She was in the bedroom for ten minutes. She came out she went straight to the bathroom in the hallway. I said, "Katie are you okay?" She didn't answer me. I figured she was mad at me. The phone was ringing, I got up from the couch and answered the phone. It was Katie's oldest daughter, Jessica. She wanted to speak to her mother. I told her, "Your mother is in the bathroom, call back!" Then I went back to sit on the couch. Katie was still in the bathroom.

All of a sudden, a thought went through my mind, she been in the bathroom about twenty minutes. I quickly got up on the couch, I was afraid! I was sweating! I ran to the bathroom saying, "Oh my God!" I knocked on the bedroom door, it was locked. I yelled, "Katie open the door!" I tried to break the door down with my shoulder, it didn't work. Then I kicked the door, and I kicked it again. I finally **broke the lock!**

I saw her on the floor next to the toilet. A needle was on the floor next to her. I was so frightened and hysterical! She was lying on her side, so I turned around so I could revive her. I was an ex-cop, so I knew what to do. I felt her pulse, there was no heartbeat. I was trying not to **throw up**. I was in shock! Katie's baby daughter was in the way. I remember pushing the baby out of my way, so I could get to the portable telephone. I got the phone and quickly, I got back to the bathroom. In my mind I knew it was too late. She had been in the bathroom too long. I tried **mouth to mouth resuscitation**, she's still not breathing. I called 911, an operator called back. I told her what happened; she was telling me what to do. I was pressing on her chest over and over. I was scared I knew the ambulance is coming by helicopter, but it's too late! The baby was yelling, "**Mommy, Mommy!**" I was starting to lose it. I told the operator "Where is the **fucken helicopter**? It's too late, she's gone!" The operator was calm and told me to try again. And I did! Over and over! The baby was crying, I was crying and saying the Lord's Prayer, "**In the Name of the Father the Son and**

the Holy Ghost." I got up and took the baby, out of the bathroom, there was no more I can do for Katie.

Finally, the helicopter arrived, they tried to revive her. It was useless, her brain had to be dead. The telephone was ringing, it was Jessica. She wanted to talk to her mother. I told her your mother had an accident, Please come home. When I was talking to Jessica, **I was totally out of my mind**. The paramedics were taking Katie to the helicopter. I went outside trying to console Jessica. She saw the paramedics taking Katie to the helicopter, she was **crying and yelling**. I grabbed her and gently put her on the grass. I told her, your mother will be okay. She was crying and trying to get to her mother! I kept her on the ground trying to comfort her.

I was shocked, when I saw David Jenkins, a longtime friend, someone must have called him up. I was happy to see him. I started to cry. I was praying to God that Katie doesn't die. I knew it was hopeless. David took me to the hospital; it was St. Mary's Hospital. It was awful to see Katie on the life supporting machine. That machine was keeping her alive. David suggested that tonight I should sleep in a motel. He stayed with me as a motel, I was completely out of control. I woke up many times **screaming** and **yelling** like a **madman**. If it wasn't for David, I never would've survived that night!

In four years, two girlfriend died on me. I'm trying to fantasize, what **the reader** is thinking about. Katie was cheating on me. Now, did I have anything to do with **Katie's death**! I am not a jealous person. Believe it or not, I didn't care if any of my girlfriends cheated on me. I hope **the reader** doesn't think that I had **Katie killed**!

The next day, we went back to the house in Cold Springs, Nevada. The Sheriff Deputies was waiting to see me. Only one of the deputies talk to me. He asked me my name and if I ever been involved with drugs. I told them, "I never used drugs and I never sold drugs!" He asked me if I knew Katie was a drug addict. I replied, "Yes I did, but I thought she was getting off drugs!" The other deputy went to the bedroom and came out with a plastic bottle. In the bottle was a white substance. I looked at the deputy and said, "I told you I don't do drugs that white substance is baby powder!"

The Sheriff's deputies stated that Katie overdosed on drugs. I know they were wrong. Katie **committed suicide**! The police didn't **believe me**, but I knew Katie didn't want to live anymore! When Katie came home that morning, she was so depressed that she could not be around guns, because she's a felon. That was a terrible shock to her. Between that terrible news and my bankruptcy, she didn't want to live anymore. She couldn't cope with all those problems. She told me many times that she didn't want to live anymore!

I want **the reader** to know what **really happened**! The police department doesn't care what really happened, just another drug addict overdosed on drugs.

That same day, Jessica called me up and asked me if I would come to the hospital. They decided to pull the cord on the life supporting machine. They had no other choice. There was no way I could see that, especially in my condition.

Dave and I went to the funeral. I was crying and completely fucked up. I knew I'll never be the same person. This was the worst tragedy of my entire life! Katie's death was a shock. I was going to adopt Katie daughter, Niki. Naturally, that never happened!

One week later, Jack, my good friend died. His car hit a telephone pole. He went home and died on the floor. I had enough of Reno, and I was fed up in my life. The Cowboy lost millions of dollars in Reno. I lost three people that were very close to me. **Do you believe this**? Windy, Katie and Jack all died in the month of May!

To the reader, were all three deaths coincident? I don't believe they were! **Do you**? Mysterious things happen in our lifetime. Do they happen for a reason? Do you believe in **the spiritual apprehension of truths** that are beyond understanding? Could a spirit be telling me to leave Reno? After Jack died, I left Reno.

I never claimed the Rolls Royce, when I filed bankruptcy. I sold it after bankruptcy was over. The only car I had left was my old truck.

I drove to Las Vegas taking all my guns, including my UZI (submachine gun). When I got to Las Vegas, the first thing I did was get an apartment. Then I got a storage unit, so I can hide my guns. I also had a silencer, (I inherited from my father) that goes along with all my arsenal. If I got caught with it, that's a federal offense!

The next day I rented a car and drove to Albuquerque, New Mexico to get my money. I went into the bank and immediately went to the safe deposit box. I took out **$500,000**. I was scared. When I got to the car, I knew I had two guns in the car. Now, I felt more comfortable. I drove back to Las Vegas. When I got there, I immediately took my gun case and put it back in the storage unit. I brought back the rental car, then I got in my truck and went to my apartment. I had $500,000; I was totally fucked up, thinking of Katie!

Three months later, it's the football season. I still have most of the money, what do you think I did? Remember, the Cowboy isn't finished gambling. I took a limousine, to the Mirage Casino, like the old days. It was a Sunday morning and I wanted to make a football bet. That is a dangerous situation for me! What do you think I did?

The reader, already knows what I did! I made three football bets at the sport casino. Would you be shocked if I told you I lost all three games! No, I guess not! I bet $100,000 on each game. So, I lost **$300,000**, more than half of what I had left. What a fucken loser! I watched all the football games at my apartment and I didn't break the television set. I have less than $200,000, which means the Cowboy is almost broke!

The year is 1996; I've been in Vegas for a year. I met someone at the MGM casino. I knew from Reno, Nevada. His name was Frank; he was involved with undesirable people! Frank asked me "What are you doing in Vegas?" I told my girlfriend died and I had to leave Reno. He knew that I was once a cop and then Chief of Police. He also knows that was a long time ago. All of a sudden, he asked I'm trying to find a bounty hunter' I was laughing, when I said, "There are hard to find and very expensive." Most of them are scumbags; believe me I know a lot about bounty hunters. They usually go after the criminals that skipped bail. Frank asked me if I would take the job I said "No, I'm going to Hawaii!" He was sad and very depressed. Frank asked me, "Why am I going to Hawaii?" I replied, "I cannot discuss that with you!"

I felt sorry for Frank, so I asked him how can I help you? After he told me what he wanted. I knew that a woman was involved and I was right! **To the reader**, this is getting interesting; someday this could **happen to you!**

He told me his wife is having an affair with a friend of his. I told him, "You don't need a bounty hunter; you need someone to beat him up!" In an angry tone of voice, he said, "How much do you want to scare him away from my wife?" Listen, Frank I don't want to do this, because someone could get killed. I want, "**$10,000** and **I hope you say no!**" Frank replied, "That's a lot of money to scare someone! What are you going to do to him?" I told him, "Don't worry I'll take care of it!"

It took me a week and the job was finished. I contacted Frank and told him the job was done. He told me to meet him at the sports bar at the MGM casino at 3 PM. When we met at the sports bar I suggested we go to the coffee shop. I told Frank everything was taken care of. I knew Frank for a long time and he is a very wealthy man. So I knew he was good for the money. **I told Frank I have a job in Hawaii**, you can pay me when I get back. Your wife's relationship with that man has ended.

A few days later I left for Maui, one of the islands of Hawaii. When I got there I got the flu. I was sick in my apartment for about a week. I called the person I was supposed to meet and told him I'll call him when I get better. He replied, no rush I'll wait to hear from you.

When I got better I met a beautiful oriental woman. She was a nice person but the bad news is she was in love with me. I knew my time in Maui was short. I had a job to do so I knew I could not start a relationship. My client was going to pay me **$50,000**. When the job was **finished** I left Maui, heading back to Las Vegas. I felt awful that I couldn't say goodbye to the woman. But, I had no other choice!

Am I confusing you? I apologize! A bounty hunter is always one step ahead of his competition. If he isn't he won't live long! I forgot to tell you all the details. I didn't want you to know; I was a amateur! Let's go back two weeks. before I left to Maui, I had to get something that was illegal! Are you shocked! I took a airplane to Denver, Colorado. Believe me I was terrified, especially of the unknown! I took a cab, from the airport and I told the cab driver to take me to the nearest DMV. I needed to find an address, to give to the DMV. After doing that, we headed to the DMV. My social security card and the address is all I need to get a driver's license. I needed a different identity! Nuturally, that's against the law! Believe me! When I went in the DMV, I was scared to death! If I get caught, I go to jail. While I was waiting in line, many thoughts went through my mind! I wanted to leave but I knew I had to get that drivers license. I was sweating and a cold chill went through my body.

Everything went ok! I left the DMV and took the cab, which was waiting for me, back to the airport. I took a deep breath and was relieved that the worst part was over!

When I got back to Las Vegas, I immediately got in touch with Bob. He was the middle man. Bob was probably a fictitious name. He gave me a phone number to call, when I got to Maui. He never gave me his name!

I took the airplane to Los Angeles. I had to change airplanes. Now I am on my way to Hawaii. It was a 6 hour trip, that didn't bother me. I felt uneasy about having a different name! If the airplane crashed, my family would never have known, that I died in an airplane crash!

When I go off the airplane, I took a cab to the hotel. It was already paid for, under my knew name. As you know I had the flu. When I called the person, I didn't know he was in Honolulu! He would meet me at the hotel. He gave me the name of the hotel the hotel was paid for. Also he would contact me on Friday! So I left Maui on Friday. Can you imagine, what I was thinking! The woman I met in Maui drove me to the airport. It took twenty minutes to get to Honolulu.

Is the reader still with me!

When I got to Honolulu. I rented a car I met the person, at my hotel, he didn't say much, just business! He gave me a paper with a name and address. Also a map and directions. He left something with me and said "When you finish, don't take this with you! I didn't say a word! I just nodded my head! The woman picked me up at the airport in Maui. To the reader I can't erase the past! I wish I could!

When I got back to Las Vegas I contacted my client and he paid me the **$50,000**, all in **hundred dollar bills**.

The next day I contacted Frank we met and he paid me **$10,000**. Therefore, I knew my job in Las Vegas was successful.

To the reader, when you are by yourself tonight, think about the word **survival**! Would you have done anything differently? Who knows what anyone is capable of doing when it comes down to surviving. The ability of the mind to know what is right or wrong. Especially, when you're in a life or death situation! **I hope this will never happen to you!**

Later in 1996, in Las Vegas. I wanted to leave the country. I could of stayed in Las Vegas and be a Bounty Hunter, but I didn't want to hurt people anymore. I already have nightmares of the "Zodiac" killer! I have $250,000 left. That's not enough to live in Costa Rica! How do I get $100,000? I don't want to be a hit man, even if I have all the equipment to become a one. Please God, Help me! I erased that thought from my mind!

To The reader:

I had special bullets that were use for combat They would cause serious damage!

If the bullet hits someone, (It was, a 45 glaze safety shell. The tip of the bullet is blue coated. The damage it did to the victim was terrifying! The bullet would shatter the bones and cause severe damage to the boy. I called those bullets the "Terminators"

The next week, I still don't have an answer to my problem. As a last resort, I can make a bet $150,000 to make $100,000 on the "Super Bowl." When I make a bet for $100,000 or more. **I lose**! If I win, I will go to Costa Rica. I didn't want to stay in Las Vegas. Therefore, I have to make the bet, so I can go to Costa Rica.

It was Saturday afternoon, the day before the Super Bowl. I was going to take a limousine to the Mirage casino. My apartment was only a mile from the Mirage casino. It's the end of a legend! The Cowboy isn't going down without a fight. The limousine let me off at the Mirage. I walked in the sports room and I put up $150,000 to win $100,000. I took Green Bay against New England in the Super Bowl. If I win I will get back $250,000. I took the limousine back to my apartment. The most money I ever won in one sport game was $80,000. I was totally shocked. I won the fucken game!

The next day, I took the same limousine to the Mirage. They paid me $250,000! When the limousine let me off at my apartment, I have $250,000 under my mattress. I should be afraid, but I'm not because I have two guns in my apartment.

Let me change the subject for a moment! **To the reader**, Let me share this with you, the legend of the Cowboy is coming to an end. From 1985 to 1996, that's 12 years of being a legend. When I was writing the story about the Cowboy. I wanted **the reader** to know what I went through! I was writing about **someone** I never **knew** also I never **met.** It was very difficult to describe a **person** that was an **adventurer**! He was always in trouble and somehow he **survived**! He was known for being a big gambler and losing millions of dollars. No one ever knew he risked his life to help others. I had a difficult time writing **about myself**! All the **hardships** and the two deaths of my girlfriends. **I couldn't write this story again**!

Let's get back to the story. I immediately got on the phone and call the airlines. I purchased two tickets for Costa Rica. One for me, the other for Dave Jenkins. He was going to come with me for a few days and then he was going back to Reno.

I call David up and told him, I got two tickets for Costa Rica. I got a passport and I will have no problem in leaving the country. David can't stay no more than a month. The scary thing is I don't speak Spanish.

David took a plane to Las Vegas and then he left the next day. The airplane stopped in Los Angeles and then in Miami. After that the airplane landed in San Jose, Costa Rica. We went to the Holiday Hotel in San Jose. I wanted to get a room and then look for an apartment. I found out if you don't speak Spanish you are in **trouble**. David left Costa Rica after three days. When he left, I was all alone, in a strange country! I didn't speak **Spanish** and hardly anybody speaks **English**. I said many times, "What the fuck am I doing here!"

Chapter XVI

End of a legend

"Cowboy" (1997 – 2001)

I met a cab driver, Rolando who spoke English, I was lucky, without him I would've left Costa Rica. The Banks, Grocery stores, Restaurants and 90 percent of the people do not speak English. I saw Rolando, six days a week and I paid him what he wanted. Rolando was my interpreter and he taught me to speak Spanish.

In 1997, I did two things. Gamble in a casino in San Jose, Costa Rica and have sex with women. The food I ate in restaurants was delicious. I liked Costa Rica much better than the United States, but the medicine was more advanced in the United States and eating inCosta Rican restaurants were expensive. I lived in Costa Rica for three years. The Costa Ricans are afraid of the Americans cause of the language problem. They also think all the Americans are rich.

Also in 1997, I had sex with many women. I don't use condoms. I am living in poor Country, without condoms, that was a mistake. Even in Costa Rica, they called me the Cowboy. I wore a cowboy hat and boots. The Cowboy wasn't scared of anything that came along. Boy was I wrong! I woke up one morning and I knew I had to see a doctor as quick as I can. Rolando took me to a Costa Rica doctor, that practiced in the United States. He took one look at my male organ, and he walked away.

He gave me a blood test and told me the bad news. I started to sweat. I had both hands over my head. I didn't want to hear what the doctors going to tell me! Slowly and calmly the doctor said, "You have **syphilis**!" When the doctor told me that, I didn't know what to say. I started to talk, I was stuttering. The doctor told me not to worry! In one week, the disease will be gone. The doctor advised me to wear a condom in Costa Rica. I told him I can't do that. Doctor smiled and said, "This is going to happen again!" I told the doctor that I'm not going to have sex anymore in Costa Rica. The doctor replied, "I hope not, for your sake!"

After that nightmare, I kept my promise; I didn't have any more sex, even with a condom. That disease, that I had, made me afraid of having sex with any woman.

In 1998, I started to run out of money. I lost a lot of money in Nevada. Now, I am losing money in Costa Rica. I am making smaller sport bets in Costa Rica, but same results.

Two months later, I had to leave Costa Rica. I didn't want to be broke in a foreign country. The two years in Costa Rica, I spent over $200,000, that's including gambling. I had a good time in Costa Rica. There was no difference between Nevada and Costa Rica. I did the same thing, and that was fucking women and losing money gambling.

So, I left Costa Rica with $10,000. I didn't know where to go, so I came back to Reno. I had enough money to survive. I got an apartment in Reno. The name of the apartments was Grant Apartments. I was so fucking depressed in my apartment. I didn't want to live anymore. I lost millions of dollars and I'm still alive, that's worse than dying. When you are by yourself, you start thinking about all the mistakes you have made. Not only I lost all my money, I lost my belief in God. After the earthquake in 1989, I hated God. It wasn't God's fault, I was fucked up.

My gambling, women and my high lifestyle of living destroyed me. I had a great time, everyone wanted to be like the Cowboy. I had a great time, but life changes. I didn't want to be a Bounty Hunter, so what do I do now! I can imagine how actors, sports players and millionaires feel when they become broke. Many of them go on living and some of them commit suicide. I am not suicidal, so I guess I am one of the few that survived.

To the reader, let me share something with you! This happen in 1998 in my apartment. Life is a mystery don't try to understand it, you will go crazy! I had enough of mental suffering and I don't want to live anymore. Also, I had nothing to live for I can only blame myself. I had a good life and now it's time to die. I had my **38 revolver** placed in my mouth, and that **hammer was cocked**. My finger was on the trigger. Quickly, a thought went through my mind. Slowly I took the revolver out of my mouth and I put the hammer down, and then I **unloaded the revolver.** I can explain why I **didn't shoot myself.** The thought that was running through my mine was of the **Zodiac Killer.** Why did that stop me from killing myself? I don't know the answer! Today, when I think of that, someone was telling me not to do it. It wasn't my time to die, but why was I thinking about the Zodiac Killer? **That's frightening**!

I got my ex-business manager phone number from my former insurance company. I called him up; he lives in West Palm Beach, Florida. He left me in 1989; I gave him $400,000 severance pay, for working for me. He told me to come to Florida; he would take care of me. I told him, let me think it over. Also I said, "I am broke!" I told him I was a bounty hunter and you know what they do. Let me call you tomorrow. I called him in the afternoon and told him, I'll buy the ticket. I will call you later. I called him back and I told him to meet me at the airport in West Palm Beach at 10 o'clock in the afternoon. He picked me up at the airport, and I stayed with him. Later I got an apartment and he paid my rent.

In 1998 through 2000 nothing much happened my friend and I went to my son's wedding in Portland, Oregon. The wedding was nice, and I got to see my son. The city of Portland was crowded and the trees were green and beautiful.

We came back to West Palm Beach, Florida. I hated it there! The humanity is awful. My friend met a woman, and he got married to a girl he just met. He married the woman, so she could take care of him. What a fucken loser he is. He told her that I was a bounty hunter! She was scared, and told him to get rid of me. If I had a gun, I would've killed both of them! I am not the **same person**! I am not the **Cowboy anymore**! I don't know who I am!

In early 2001 they were plotting against me, so they purchased a ticket for me to leave, so I could go back to Reno. I was thinking they were going to kill me!His wife was an ugly woman, and a vicious lady. I told him someday I will be back. I just walked away, he knew if I ever came back he is a dead man.

I took the airplane back to Reno, Nevada. I was thinking that I was lucky. I believe the woman told my friend to kill me before I left West Palm Beach, they invited me to dinner. I didn't go because I was scared they were trying to poison me! On the airplane I had a lot of time to think. They were scared of me coming back to kill them! When a woman knows a man has $400,000 in a safe deposit box, somehow she is going to get that money!

Cowboy: The Legend

Let's get back to why she wants me dead! This is easy to understand. I am the only one that could stop her. When I got off the plane in Reno, I was all fucked up. I remember David driving me from the airport to the Silver Club in Sparks Nevada. That day he got me a room at the hotel. The next day I went to the Grant apartments in south Reno and rented a room.

To the reader the cowboy had one more **horrifying event** that happened to him, you will learn how most people are **pathetic**.

Are you ready? I was in the room about an hour, when I got a phone call from a friend in Carson City Nevada. He asked me if I had a good trip. I was sweating and thoughts were running through my mind. Why is he calling me? I tried to be calm like nothing happened. He continued to say "I need your help!" I tried to keep my composure. But I couldn't! Mike, how can I help you? In a sad tone of voice, he said "**I can't take it anymore I want you to kill my wife!**" I will give you **$100,000**! He started to cry and was begging me to help him! I was standing up while I was talking to him. Now, I had to sit down on my bed. I was stunned! I told him "**I was a bounty hunter, not a killer!**" I could hear him crying. I hung up the phone, shaking my head, wondering if he was telling me the truth. The phone rang again, it was Mike. He said, Ray, I'm scared "I don't know what to do. My wife is going to take all of my money. "We can't talk on the phone about this anymore. I hung up and we were going to meet the next day.

The next day we met at a coffee shop. I told him I'm sorry but I don't do this **anymore**. You'll have to find someone else. He asked me if I knew of anybody. I told him I didn't know of anyone. Before we left the coffee shop I told him this conversation never happened.

To the reader, in 1996 I was a bounty hunter and did something I shouldn't have done. I'm a different person today. We all make mistakes in life. Probably you wouldn't have done the same thing I did in 1996. Who knows what a person will do in a **life or death situation**.

In 2001, I drove to Tucson, Arizona. My daughter Pam was getting married. I enjoyed the wedding and I got to see my daughter. It's been nine years since I saw her.

Also in 2001, in Reno I changed my name to **Gino Valentino.** Gino was my nickname in Las Vegas and a long time ago I knew a young man, that was killed in Vietnam. His name was Valentino. So **the legend** of a man, that had everything **has ended**.

Chapter XVII

Zodiac Investigations

(2002 – 2009)

I tried everything in my power to solve the " Zodiac" case. The San Francisco and Vallejo Police Departments was **pathetic**. In my opinion the San Francisco Chronicle staff writers were **incompetent**! There were **two "Zodiac" killers.** That's why the police departments didn't catch the "Zodiac" killer. My investigations will prove who the "Zodiac" was! I was a policeman for six years. I was involved with the "Zodiac" for two years. Therefore, almost half the time I was a policeman, I was involved with the "Zodiac" serial killers! That is **unbelievable**! I would like **the reader** to decide and make **their own decision.**

In 2002, I truly believe Wayne Messier was the "Zodiac" killer. But I had to prove it. At that time, I was living in Reno, Nevada. Me and my friend, Don drove to Colma, California. Hoping to find information. We went to Mercy Ambulance that is where Wayne Messier worked and lived. We found out the building is still there, but Mercy Ambulance went out of business. It was located next to the Colma Fire Department.

Later we drove to the Broadmoor Police Department (Broadmoor is unincorporated Colma), trying to get information on Lt. Merrill Baxley. They told us they have no record on Baxley and they never heard of him. I was shocked and very angry, all that day was disappointing and I didn't know what else to do.

Later that night, I was so depressed from all the memories of the

"Zodiac." Thinking about that day when I was forced to bury the woman. I was ashamed of myself. How could I do something so hideous! Carrying the woman's body and placing it in the grave. When I think of that night I start crying and I can't stop. My only salvation is to solve the "Zodiac" case, so **Donna Lass can rest in peace forever.**

The next day he drove to Reno, Nevada. I got the phone number of Lt. Baxley from a friend. I called Mr. Baxley and he was shocked that I called him. Baxley told me that Mr. MacDonald, who was the owner of Mercy Ambulance and Police Commissioner of Broadmoor Police, told him one of his ambulance drivers was bragging to his co - workers that he hunted people and talking about "Satan." I already knew all the information that Baxley told me! Also, Baxley stated that Messier and his roommate was arrested by San Francisco inspector Dave Toschi in 1967, but Messier was not booked. Unexpectedly, Baxley got very angry and hung up on me. I immediately called back, Baxley answered and then hung up again. That was the last time I called Mr. Baxley!

Later on, through the mail I received Wayne Messier's death certificate. This information will further prove that Wayne was the "Zodiac" killer. The San Francisco police file dated the "Zodiac's" birthday was the end of December and "Zodiac" was an engineer. Wayne Messier was an engineer and was born on December 29, 1941.

Also that day, I called the two private detectives in Sacramento, California , to see if I could get a photo of Wayne Messier. One of the detectives was a retired FBI agent. He told me that getting a photo of someone from 37 years ago is very difficult to get. He also stated it would cost a lot of money. Again, I fail and I became emotionally drained, but I continued on.

The next week I go to Sacramento, California. I knew Wayne went to high school in the Sacramento area, but I didn't know if that high school exists today. The only other thing I could think of is maybe the department of motor vehicle could help me. Well, I was wrong! They told me after so many years, all the photos are destroyed. Just another failure, I drove back to Reno, Nevada.

In 2002, I contacted through the Internet, a private investigator that was working for Donna's Lass's sister. I told the investigator that I was a police officer in 1970 and I had information regarding Donna Lass. I was trying to console Donna's Lass sister, but there was no response.

San Francisco Police Department described "Zodiac" as ambidextrous and also walked with a limp. The police stated that "Zodiac" was a Satan worshiper, acquainted with the First Church of Satan in San Francisco. Wayne was ambidextrous and he walked with a limp. Also Wayne belonged to the Satan Church in San Francisco. Vallejo Police Department stated that "Zodiac" was driving a white Chevy Impala. (Wayne drove a white Chevy Impala). The most important factor of my investigation was, when Wayne Messier left for Los Angeles in 1971. The "Zodiac" killings stopped.

I couldn't find a photo of Wayne Messier and also I couldn't prove he worked for Mercy Ambulance. I got the phone number of an ambulance company in Sacramento, California. They bought Mercy Ambulance. I called them and they don't have any records on Mercy Ambulance. Just another disappointment!

The next week I contacted the San Francisco Chronicle staff writer through his e-mail. I notified him that I was a rookie police officer in 1970 and was involved with the killer who I found out later was the "Zodiac" killer. There was no response.

In 2007 two men came to where I was working. One of the men showed me a San Francisco police badge. I was working at the thrift shop on fourth Street in Reno, Nevada. I know what they wanted, so we all went outside the store to talk. I assumed they were police officers, both men wore civilian clothes. One of the officers asked me if I knew Raymond Ottoboni(my birth name), I immediately answered," No, I don't!" He replied, "Do you know where he is?" I started to stutter and then slowly I replied, "I think I know where he is, why do you want to see him?"

The officer stated it was a personal matter. I told the officer that I would tell Ray, that the San Francisco police were at the thrift shop, and they want to talk to you! They left in an unmarked police vehicle. That was the last time I saw them. Why would the San Francisco police come to Reno, Nevada? Who gave them the name Raymond Ottoboni? Remember, I changed my name in 2001. They thought they were talking to Gino (that name was on my name tag). I always wondered why they didn't come back.

Two weeks later, I was driving into my storage unit,(Evans & McCarran) when I noticed a vehicle parked on the other side of the roadway. It was an **unmarked police vehicle.** As I drove through the gate, I knew that I was being followed! I wasn't scared because I already knew what they wanted. I waited for an hour thinking, "What the hell do I do now?" All the time I was thinking, "Am I going to be killed?" I definitely knew they were undercover police officers. They were either **San Francisco policemen or FBI agents**.

I finally left the storage unit, **the unmarked police vehicle was still there**. I drove southbound on Evans. In my rearview mirror I observed the police vehicle following me. I had a 38. Revolver in my vehicle, but I quickly erased that thought from my mind. I turned right at the intersection of Evans and 6th, and then a left on Lake Street. Again I looked in my rearview mirror and the unmarked police vehicle disappeared! Thank God! I knew this "cat and mouse" game had to stop! I thought of filing a complaint with the Reno Police Department, but I change my mind.

To my knowledge, they have never followed me again! I believe they thought the story I had was made up! **Wrong**!

A month later, I was staying at the Motel 6 on Victorian Avenue in Sparks, Nevada. At approximately 3 PM in the afternoon, there was a knock on the front door. I opened the door and there were two men (both of them wore suits). One of the men asked me if my name was Gino Valentino. I replied, "**Yes, it is. Who are you?**" There was no response and everything became silent. In an angry tone of voice I **yelled**," Leave me alone! **Who are you Fucking guys?**" It was like they lost their voice, both men walked away. I was frightened, as I closed the motel door, I was thinking about whether or not my life was in danger. I never found out who they were. They look like cops, but whoever they were; I'm convinced they were looking for information on the "**Zodiac**."

After going to all the terrifying events in 2007, I was thinking of going to the FBI office in Reno, Nevada, and notify them of the information I have on the "Zodiac" killers! I was scared, so I decided not to go.

Getting back to Messier, he went from an engineer to an ambulance driver in Colma, a cemetery town! That's unbelievable! Something is wrong, Wayne knew he had a fatal disease and went berserk. He must've quit or got fired from his job. I'm not talking about a normal person here, not only is he a Satan worshiper, also his idol was Charles Manson. Remember, I didn't know all this information in 1970.

In 1970 Wayne told me numerous times about his friend, whom I never met, and his name was "Hoss". I never thought anything unusual about that name. In 2007, during my investigation I found out that's the Nick name of Arthur Leigh Allen. Allen's face and body were very similar to Dan Blocker, who starred in the TV show Bonanza. I don't know if Wayne ever knew Alan, but he could have.

In all the years I knew Wayne Messier, I never saw him with a woman, in fact he hated women. Messier's death certificate stated that he was married. I was totally confused and I didn't believe that he was married. A week later, I found out through the Internet, that Messier married Elaine Klotchman on September 10, 1972, in Los Angeles, three months before he died in December 11, 1972.

Let's look at all the information I have on Wilford Messier. Wilford rushed his son's body from Los Angeles to Sacramento the very next day to be buried. Why so fast? His son was nobody, or was he? Wilford was the owner of a white Chevy Impala that was driving through Vallejo during the late 1960s. Wilford was a military man, which is why Wayne wore a military outfit (wing walkers) when he went shooting at my fathers range. And finally Wilford was the owner of the car that Wayne drove in Lake Tahoe with the body of Donna Lass.

Now, did Wilford know that his son was going to kill Donna Lass? And did Wilford own the house in Lake Tahoe were Donna Lass's body was brought? In 1972 Wayne told me on the telephone that his father Wilford was in Santa Rosa visiting a friend. Five women were killed in Santa Rosa in 1972. Most of them there were killed by strangulation, with a rope tied in a knot. Wilford was very skillful in tying knots! Obviously, there were two serial killers!Who owned the house and Broadmoor? It wasn't Wayne. We will never know all the answers!

I contacted the Department of Defense regarding information of getting a photo of Wilford Messier. I was informed they cannot give out any information because I was not family or related in any way.

Wayne Messier and his father are buried at Mount Vernon Cemetery in Fair Oaks, California. Where is Helen Messier, which is the mother of Wayne and how come she is not buried with Wayne and Wilford? (I found out in December of 2009 that Helen Messier died. She was never buried with her husband and son.) Why? Did she know something about the Zodiacs!

How did I come to the conclusion that **two "Zodiac's"** In 1968 to 1972 there were two serial killers stalking and killing their victims in different methods. **This isn't my opinion! This is fact!** One killer using guns and knives or a bayonet and the other killer using his hands.(Torturing and strangling his victims with a clothesline tied in a knot.) Wayne couldn't commit those crimes in 1972. He was dying in a Los Angeles hospital. I believe he father killed the five women in Santa Rosa, California. In the last 150 years, there is never been a **father and son serial killers** in the United States. **That is frightening**!

To the reader, what do you think? I solved the Zodiac case. A DNA test will prove that I am right.

"Zodiac" made San Francisco and Vallejo Police Department looked like amateurs. When San Francisco and Vallejo receive my letters, why didn't they contact me? Obviously, they were scared; they thought I knew something that would solve the "Zodiac"case.

Let us go and see why the San Francisco and Vallejo Police Department's failed. Both Police Department wanted to solve the crime themselves. The "Zodiac" played cat and mouse with the police departments through the newspaper. The FBI entered the " Zodiac" case in 1970 because of the murder of Donna Lass. They were puzzled by the "Zodiac's" cryptograms. In 1992 the FBI closed its files on the "Zodiac" investigation.

In 2002, the San Francisco Police Department cleared Arthur Leigh Allen through DNA evidence.

DNA CLEARS ZODIAC SUSPECT

Unthinkable, that a **detective from Broadmoor police department** and a **rookie cop** from **Colma Police Department** would solve the most important crime in **California history**. I give credit to MerrillBaxley for the work he did, and for me I just happened to be in the wrong place at the wrong time!

In August of 2007, I was **warned not to write this story**. John Harrison, a retired San Francisco police officer, now working as a security officer at a Nevada casino, showed **deep concern for my safety**. He told me the "Zodiac" is the most important crime in California history. The San Francisco Police Department was disgraced.

The next weekend I saw John Harrison in the Nevada casino, and we talked again about the "Zodiac" killer. After warning me last week not to write the story, he told me about an incident that happened to him when he was a rookie with San Francisco Police Department in 1973. He was at the scene of a murder at Golden gate Park in San Francisco. The victim was shot and killed by sniper. In a serious tone of voice he told me about how the San Francisco Police Department was afraid when the movie Magnum force came out. I realize what he was trying to tell me. The movie "Magnum Force" starring Clint Eastwood, was about four San Francisco police officers, on motorcycles, killing any criminals that came in their path. **They were vigilantes!**

The public who saw this movie really thought the movie was fiction, if they only knew they were wrong! Mr. Harrison knew who killed the victim. It was a San Francisco Police Officer. Mr. Harrison told me he knew him, the killer was one of the 12 that hunts down guilty suspects that the judge or jury let go on a technicality. Mr. Harrison was happy because that person will never kill again. After Mr. Harrison told me this I was frightened and couldn't believe that a Police Department would do something this hideous. When we finished talking I immediately went to the casino restroom and threw up. Also, Mr. Harrison told me I would be arrested on a warrant and then I **would disappear.** After he told me this I was sweating and terrified. **But I had to write this story. No matter what happens!**

One week later I went back to the Casino to see Mr. Harrison. I found out Mr. Harrison quit his job, without giving any notice. I was frightened, and I didn't go to work. I knew why he quit. Finally, **Mr. Harrison realized he shouldn't have given me that information.** To this day, I don't know where Mr. Harrison is.

Vallejo Police Department was totally confused. Their main suspect was Arthur Leigh Allen. Allen was in trouble most of his life with different police departments. Allen was arrested by Vallejo police in 1958 for disturbing the peace. Two days later he was released. Santa Rosa police arrested Allen in 1974 for child molesting. He was sentenced to Atascadero State Hospital for the criminally insane for felony child molesting. He served two years and 15 days. When Allen got out of Atascadero State Hospital he was sent to Sonoma County jail and served 150 days. None of these crimes are pertaining to murder or any human sacrificing (Satanic). **Allen was not a violent person. Allen died in August 1992. San Francisco homicide inspectors cleared Allen through DNA evidence in 2002. Inspectors Kelly Carroll and Michael Maloney's stated that Allen did not match the DNA fingerprint development from bonafide "Zodiac" letters.**

I did anything of my power to solve the "Zodiac" case for the public but San Francisco and Vallejo police did absolutely nothing. After I gave them information on Messier in a certified letter, San Francisco and Vallejo Police Department fucked-up the "Zodiac" case from the beginning to the end. **Today, the San Francisco police believe there were two "Zodiacs" functioning as a team one killing and the other writing to the newspaper. Finally, the San Francisco police are getting smart! There were two "Zodiacs" functioning as a team both "Zodiacs" were killers!**

In 1991, the San Francisco Examiner newspaper interviewed Allen. He claimed he received a letter from the Department of Justice clarifying that he wasn't the "Zodiac." Also Allen stated that Vallejo police seized the letter when they raided his house in 1991. Vallejo police wanted Allen to be the killer even if he was innocent.

I believe that Bruce Davis,(hit man of Charles Manson) was involved with the "Zodiac" killer. In the late 1990's a private detective was investigating Bruce Davis. He found out that Davis's FBI files were locked up in a special vault, so that no one could get to them. What is FBI trying to hide? Could it be about what happened in Lake Tahoe in 1970! The FBI is hiding Bruce Davis, because they know Bruce was involved with the "Zodiac" Remember, I was there in Lake Tahoe with Bruce Davis and Messier. Bruce Davis aka Bruce McMillan is now serving a life sentence at San Luis Obispo, California. He killed two people in 1969.(Charles Manson killings) Davis surrendered to Los Angeles police on December 2, 1970. Davis was seen in the San Francisco area in the autumn of 1970, he killed approximately five people for Charles Manson. He was a Satan worshiper and today he is a born again Christian.

Bruce Davis, and Wayne Messier lived in Sacramento, California in 1964. Both disappeared in 1965! **Bruce Davis was a proven killer with a fascination for occult symbolism.** Davis and Messier were both Satan worshipers. Did they meet at the Satan church in San Francisco? **Both parties were living in San Francisco in the late 1960s. Were they roommates?** Bruce Davis's fingerprints didn't match those alleged to be the zodiac killer. Wayne Messier was arrested in San Francisco with his roommate in 1966 or 1967. **Was his roommate Bruce Davis? I believe he was! Bruce Davis moved from San Francisco the same time Wayne Messier moved out!** During my research on Bruce Davis, I found out that information from the San Francisco telephone directory! **To the reader**, now, do you believe that **Bruce Davis was involved** with the "Zodiac" killer?

In June of 2002, Don my friend, also mailed certified letters to San Francisco and Vallejo Police Department's about information concerning the "Zodiac" killer and me. I stated in the letter that I could prove the "Zodiac" is Wayne Messier. The letter mentioned that I was formally Chief of Police of Colma, California. They could care less. The return certified letters were signed by **San Francisco** and **Vallejo Police Departments. There was no response!**

The Police Departments failed me. They failed the system. The San Francisco Police Department is a disgrace to the city. The most **important unsolved crime** in San Francisco history, and they do not care if they ever solve the case! **I lost respect** for the San Francisco and Vallejo Police

Department in the 1970's. Can you imagine what respect I have for them today?

As a former chief of police, from the Bay Area, I know that the "Zodiac" case is very popular today. The police departments, that are involved in solving the "Zodiac" case should have given their best effort, even after 38 years. It still can be solved today, especially by the information I have.

I know this is a cold case, but this is the famous "Zodiac" serial killer. The public has a right to know who the Zodiac was! Today, when I think about San Francisco and Vallejo Police Department, I get sick to my stomach. What was the main reason they did not contact me? I know the question will never be answered. **I pray every day in memory of the "Zodiac"victims.**

I didn't kill Donna Lass, I had no knowledge that she was going to be killed before that fatal Sunday morning. I had never met Donna Lass. The only time I saw the name Donna Lass was on a poster at South Lake Tahoe Police Station in 1970. I felt responsible for her death, because I drove Wayne Messier to Lake Tahoe. All these years I felt guilty of depriving the parents of Donna Lass of never seeing their daughter's gravesite. That will haunt me forever! I can't change what happened. But I owe it to the family of Donna Lass to tell what happened in Lake Tahoe in 1970 and also to disclose who killed her. No matter what the consequences will be!

In 2008, I found an abundance of information about serial killers. They are completely different from ordinary killers. You will never recognize a serial killer. He would appear to be normal, or married with family. How could I had any reason to know that Wayne or his father were serial killers. Let us think back in time to the 1970's. When I met Wayne, on the job. I had no reason to think he was a killer, let alone a serial killer. At the restaurants, shooting range, etc., he was not normal, an eccentric person, and acting weird! Again, I had no reason to think he was the "Zodiac" serial killer. After all the information I had in the 1970's. I finally realized Wayne could be the "Zodiac" killer. My experience as a police officer was limited, so I did not continue to look for any more information on Wayne or his father. That was my critical mistake! I did not have the information I have now.

Wayne grew up in Sacramento, California. He went to high school and studied to be an engineer. The death certificate stated he was an engineer with the State of California for nine years. That is a lie! After all the information I have there is no way, Wayne worked nine years with the Highway Department! Why did Wayne go to Colma, California and worked as an ambulance driver? **He went from an engineer to an ambulance driver. That is unbelievable!** Remember, Wayne had a fatal disease and knowing that he was going to die did not keep him from doing something very evil, like killing! Wayne was a Satan worshiper and treated people like slaves, just as the "Zodiac" did.

The "Zodiac" killed always on or next to a holiday, and he was obsessed by water. Four "Zodiac" killings were next to water. Two were in Vallejo; the other two were in Lake Berryessa and Lake Tahoe. "Zodiac II" was very different. He was killing with his hands; also, he was killing in rural areas. There were no guns or knives involved in his crimes. His motive was revenge. He wasn't a copycat!

When I mention the name, Wilfred Messier. I get scared to death. Wilfred was the owner of everything that was involved in the zodiac killings. Does that make them accomplish? In my opinion, yes he was! In 1970, at the shooting range, there was a problem with one of the target holders. Wilfred fixed the problem by tie a piece of cord in a knot. He had a special knowledge of tying knots.

There's one thing that bothers me. Let us go back to Lake Tahoe in 1970. I don't believe Bruce Davis helped Wayne kill Donna Lass. Wilfred's vehicle was used in the transportation of Donna Lass's body. That was the same vehicle (white Chevy Impala) driving through Vallejo in 1968 –1969. **It's impossible to ascertain which serial Killer murdered first!** That is why the zodiac case was so difficult. **The police departments were looking for one serial killer. That is why they failed.**

In 1969/1970, Wilfred was a patient of Letterman Hospital in San Francisco. The hospital is located in the Presidio (military base). Donna Lass worked as a nurse at Letterman Hospital in 1969/1970. One of the **Messiers** met her, something must have happened! That's why **she was killed?**

I never investigated Wilfred Messier is in the 1970's. I should have, but I was too busy watching Wayne. Wilfred was a catalyst in Wayne killing. I believe Wilfred was scared of his son being caught as the "Zodiac" killer.. There were hideous crimes that Wayne was incapable of doing. Obviously, there were **two "Zodiac."**

To the reader, The "Zodiac"case will never be solved by the Police Department. They don't care anymore. It is up to you the reader to solve it! I know you already solved it!

Wilfred was in the Vallejo and Sacramento area in 1970. Five women were tortured and strangled with a closesline in Santa Rosa California. In

1972, Wilfred lived in Sonoma, which is next to Santa Rosa. Five women were strangled and beaten with a clothesline tied in a knot. Wilford fits the description of how those women were killed. Wayne fits the description of the six killings (3 in Vallejo, one each at Lake Berryessa, San Francisco and Lake Tahoe). Wayne killed by guns and bayonet. Also **there is the possibility that Wilfred started killing before his son**! Lake Tahoe killing was different it was personal! **Believe me I know**! No matter how bizarre it sounds, it is very difficult to obtain any physical evidence, especially when the killings occurred 41 years ago. All the Police Departments that were involved. No one ever contacted me, to see what information I had. If they did, **the "Zodiac case" would of been solved**!

This is the first case of a **father and son serial killer team** in the United States. Could I be mistaken? No! Wayne, I truly believe was the "Zodiac killer." He warned me about his father on the phone in 1972. Wayne was dying and he had no reason to lie! They killed in different ways that is why the Police Departments were very confused!

Let us talk about the Santa Rosa, Police Department in California. The five women that were killed in 1972, all the women were killed by either strangulation by a rope or they were beaten to death. Santa Rosa Police Department never had a suspect; they believe one man, a military man, skillful in tying knots, committed those crimes. Wilfred Messier was in the military, and as you know, he was very skillful in tying knots. **It has been 38 years since the murder of those women in Santa Rosa. It has never been solved!**

Santa Rosa Police Department is very confused by the serial killer. In 2009 I found out vital information that proves my investigation on the Santa Rosa killing in 1972. The Police Department **finally realizes the "Zodiac" killer** committed those killings. They were confused because the killings were not done in the "Zodiac" style of killing. They were **right**! "Zodiac" did not kill those victims; **it was "Zodiac II."**

Later that year, I discovered information that confused me. After 1972 the Santa Rosa killings continued. A serial killer was still killing young women by strangulation. The mystery of Zodiac ll continues!

Also in 2009, I found out vital information convincing me that Wayne Messier was the <u>"Zodiac" Killer</u>!" The San Francisco police department stated that the "Zodiac Killer complained, over the telephone, that he was suffering from terrible headaches! Wayne Messier suffered from migraine headache! To the reader, you must know by now I have <u>solved</u> this case!

I know what you are thinking! I can't prove it, but a DNA test can!

Let us go back a year. In October 2008, I took a trip to my hometown Colma, California. I went to see the new Colma Police Station. It look fabulous! It is located across the street from the Colma Town Hall. I started thinking back in time. It was 1970 and was at my father's shooting range, which is still there today. I was thinking of Bruce Davis, Wayne Messier, and Joey C. While I was thinking, I started to sweat and a cold chill went through my body. That day there was three killers and a rookie police officer at the shooting range. As I continue walking, I started to think about Joey C., is he alive? Is he in jail? I don't ever want to see Joey C.! Yes, I am scared of Joe C. He would kill me if he ever found out I mentioned his name! Quickly, I erased that thought from my mind.

As I stand here on a beautiful sunny day in 2008, at Mount Vernon Memorial Cemetery in Fair Oaks. California. Looking down at the **two adjacent graves** with tears streaming down my cheeks I am wishing that I could go back in time knowing what I know now, **I would have kill them both myself**. I am walking away for the final time. I was very angry, telling myself over and over **"I let them get away!"**

In conclusion, I left out vital information about my "Zodiac" investigations. I didn't write about the woman who was extremely involved with the "Zodiac" killers I was advised by legal constraints not to write about this person, even if she was involved with the "Zodiac" killers! I had no other choice!

Chapter XVIII

Published Book

"End of Zodiac" (2009 – 2010)

In July of 2009, I published a book called "End of Zodiac." It **was based on a true story** about my involvement with the "Zodiac" killer. Writing this book wasn't easy. Not only did I have to find witnesses, I had to research for information. The book has facts that **actually happened!** In fact, there were two "Zodiac" killers (father and son). After my book was published, different people came out in public, and wrote a book they also knew the "Zodiac" was! All the publicity they got destroyed my book! I wrote this book for **closure for myself and "Zodiac" victims.** Whoever wrote those other books did so for frame and fortune.

Today, in 2010 the "Zodiac" killer **has never been solved!** The Police Departments, who was involved in the "Zodiac" case, does not want to solve the case. **Including the FBI! Why is that?**

When I mention the victims of the "Zodiac" killers, I feel **good about myself.** I am positive I found their killers and that makes me feel good.

This is the last chapter of my book. There wasn't a dull moment in my life. **There is one mystery, I will never understand.** Maybe you could help me solve that **puzzling mystery.** It will bother me the rest of my life. **To the reader,** in **2009/2010, I sent a certified letter to the FBI, and I gave them my book.** The next day I mailed a certified letter to the El Dorado Sheriff's Office in California. Also I gave them my book. That is where Donna Lass was missing! I also mailed a certified letter, with my book, to the Tahoe Daily Tribune newspaper in

California. That is the newspaper, where Donna Lass was missing. **None of those agencies contacted me.**

In 2009, two people disappeared, they were going to help me find information about the "Zodiac" Killer. I never saw them again! I believe somebody scared them. Was the FBI involved! One person was a scriptwriter and the other person was working for me, regarding the "Zodiac" case!

How could all these events happen to one individual?

In 1970, I was involved with a serial killer! In 1972 I was involve with the mob! 1976, I was arrested for vote fraud! In 1980, I won the town election. It was the biggest comeback in Northern California! That was the happiest day of my life. In 1986, I was under surveillance by the FBI, they didn't have enough information to arrest me! Also in 1986, I became a bounty hunter against pimps! Later in 1996, I was a full-time bounty hunter. in 2009, I mailed my book "End of Zodiac" to the FBI. I committed a crime. I guess they didn't believe me! I was very lucky!

All these amazing events that happened to me. I got my revenge from all my enemies and I succeeded in avoiding danger to myself. Was it just luck, or was I more clever than my opponents! What do you think!

The only answer to this mystery is someone didn't want me to <u>solve</u> the Zodiac" case!

To the reader, finally, I am finished talking about Police Department. **I have no respect for them**! I am totally lost! I contacted four Police Departments, three Newspapers. Every agency was involved with the!"Zodiac"case! The "Zodiac" case was the **most famous unsolved crime in California! Could there been a police cover-up? Are you the reader shocked? This is unbelievable! What was your conclusion?** No matter what it was! I will respect your opinion!

To The Reader

I hope you enjoyed this true story of my life. I had to write this book, I knew you would like it! There was plenty of **suspense and shocking events** that were terrifying! I made a lot of mistakes, but no one is perfect. Only "God" has a right to judge me. I will understand if you dislike me, sometimes I hate myself. Most of the situations in my life, I had no control of! **I like the idea of talking to you during the entire story.** After reading many books, I never seen this procedure in any autobiography book. I kept you involved throughout the story. That gave me more inspiration to write this story . **The Legend of the Cowboy is gone**, but they never will forget him! I like to thank **the reader,** for having the **patience dealing** with my never ending problems. **It's been fun**!